Nancy Capistran, PCC, CPC

OPEN YOUR EYES
AND *LEAD*

Hardship and wisdom shape the best leaders in life

Eclipse
Publishing & Media

OPEN YOUR EYES
AND *LEAD*

Hardship and wisdom shape the best leaders in life

Nancy Capistran, PCC, CPC

"911" for senior-level leaders

© 2018 Nancy Capistran

First published in the United States of America in 2018 by
Eclipse Publishing & Media Ltd
22 Hillcrest
Tunbridge Wells
Kent TN4 0AJ

www.epmbooks.co.uk

Disclaimer
The author and publisher believe that the sources of information upon which
this book is based are reliable and have made every effort to ensure the accuracy
of the text. However, neither the publisher nor the author can accept any
legal responsibility whatsoever for consequences that may arise from errors or
omissions, or from any opinion or advice given.

ISBN 978-1-912839-00-1 (paperback)
ISBN 978-1-912839-50-6 (ebook)

Substantive editing by Tobe Gerard
Cover design by Aimée Coveney
Copy-edited by Graham Hughes
Text design by Daisy Editorial

Printed in the US by Data Reproductions Corporation, Auburn Hills, Michigan
Distributed by US: SCB Distributors
            UK: Roundhouse Group

Contents

Endorsements

"A quote attributed to President John F. Kennedy states, 'Change is the law of life. And those who look only to the past or present are certain to miss the future.' There are always changes in one's life by choice or dictated by others. *Open Your Eyes and* LEAD reinforces that we are, in fact, the leaders of our own life and not the victim of our circumstances. The way we choose to show up and react to our own personal and professional challenges will have a major impact on our brand and future success. I recommend this book to anyone who feels that their life's challenges are negatively impacting the achievement of their goals."

– Dr. Edward Lacerte, former Athletic Trainer and Physical Therapist, Boston Celtics; President, ProSports Therapy

"Through *Open Your Eyes and* LEAD, Nancy Capistran has given us a true masterpiece of what 'leadership' is and should look like. Graciously sharing some real-life personal and professional challenges, as well as victories, she helps open her readers' eyes to new leadership possibilities. Her book is comprehensive, but not complex, and will resonate with readers who seek to abandon status quo… a must-read!!!"

– M.L. Carr, former two-time world champion Boston Celtics player, Head Coach, and General Manager

"The real-life stories in *Open Your Eyes and* LEAD are interesting and inspiring. There are great ideas on how each of us can choose to handle our personal and professional challenges with examples of processes that turned these critical moments into success and positive learning experiences. Great insights for living a better life."

– Michael Cote, President and CEO, Secureworks

"Nancy has been on the front lines of many of life's most formidable challenges. Her remarkable ability to not only survive but thrive as a result of those challenges has given her a depth and breadth of skills that she shares with her readers in *Open Your Eyes and* LEAD. The book combines personal and professional stories from the trenches, along with Nancy's unique brand of insight and wisdom that enables readers to identify and create their own profound ripple effect of change. This book is a must-read for those who want to understand how to turn their life's struggles into a positive outcome for themselves and the many people they touch."

– Dr. Jessica Erdmann-Sager, Plastic and Reconstructive Surgeon at Brigham & Women's Hospital and an Instructor in Surgery, Harvard Medical School

"Leadership, whether in business, community, family, or sports is the fundamental driver of success. Through "Open Your Eyes and LEAD", Nancy gives us a leadership model that leads to excellence in today's world of uncertainty. Equal parts art and science, this book shows how to rise to the occasion when heat is on. As a coach to some of the world's top athletes the lessons and inspirational stories learned in this book are a game changer."

– Ben Bergeron, CrossFit Level-4 Coach, Coach of 7 CrossFit Games Championships, Best-Selling Author

"Nancy Capistran's *Open Your Eyes and* LEAD offers us a new way to embrace a strategic change in how we think about leadership and our leaders today. Nancy's straight talk on how to create a positive and diverse work culture mirrors our firm's goals – as an international law firm with a strong set of core values – and, importantly, helps to set a path on how to achieve them. Drawing on her professional and personal experience, Capistran's 'in the trenches' writing style is refreshing. I found myself underlining numerous passages that will help me become a better leader within my own practice group at the firm and advisor to my clients, and that I'm sure will aid me in my personal life as well."

– Lewis Segall, Corporate Law Partner and Leader of the Corporate/Mergers & Acquisitions Group, Sullivan & Worcester; published author

"*Open Your Eyes and* LEAD is a roadmap to better understand why we don't always show up as our best selves in challenging circumstances. The author provides actionable steps to strengthen our resolve and to achieve better outcomes. It's a must-read for those who want to improve their leadership capabilities."

– Willie O'Reilly, Columnist, Sunday Business Post (Ireland)

"Capistran does amazing work and has captured the essence of leadership. Not only does she highlight her own personal and professional stories of managing through adversity, she shares the struggles of dozens of colleagues and clients who have overcome their own personal and professional gremlins. If you want to become a better, stronger and more empathetic leader, read this book."

– Ted Clark, Northeastern University: Director, Center for Family Business; Executive Professor Entrepreneurship and Innovation

Foreword

As a New England Patriots player for my entire NFL career, I've had the privilege of working with and being mentored by several incredible leaders, each of whom has played a role in my success.

I've witnessed exceptional leadership both on and off the field that inspired teams and people to greatness, enabling them to achieve incredible success despite the odds.

In the game of football to become a better player, a better teammate and a better person, I learned that you have to practice all the time. There are no shortcuts to being great. That's the Patriot way and while it applies to football, it also applies to everyday life. Whatever role you play, do it to the best of your ability, because it has a ripple effect on the people around you as it makes you better.

I've also learned to never underestimate the power of a great coach. During my career, I've had several – from Bill Parcells to Pete Carroll to Bill Belichick. Each of these men inspired and helped me in a different way.

For more than 30 years, Nancy Capistran has inspired senior-level leaders from start-ups to multibillion-dollar enterprises to weather storms, recognize blind spots and create positive change in their companies, in their relationships, and in the world around them.

Open Your Eyes and LEAD shows readers how to become a positive influence in the world, and how to balance and manage issues they face as they strive for excellence in all they do and remain true to their core beliefs even when it's easier not to.

One of the things that struck me deeply was Capistran's acknowledgment that we all have moments of self-doubt and face adversity in some way; but it's how we respond to those situations that makes us who we are.

No one gets through life without a major challenge or two, and Capistran candidly shares and explores her own extreme and unpredictable life experiences that have impacted both her and her family on a profound level. What I admire most about Nancy is that she stepped up and showed up during tough times. Nancy's ability to remain positive through these challenges has helped her develop street-smart approaches that enabled her to thrive through adversity and guide others.

Whether you are a seasoned leader, a newly minted entrepreneur, or an aspiring leader, Capistran's stories of inspiration and advice resonate with everyone who wants to increase their self-confidence, improve performance, and become a more balanced, thoughtful leader.

The book's narrative empowers readers to identify their own personal weaknesses, create workarounds to roadblocks, and persevere despite the odds.

Leadership is a highly intentional act. *Open Your Eyes and* LEAD reminds us that no matter where we are in life, we always have the power to make a positive change to improve our own lives and the lives of the people around us.

– Troy Brown, Foxboro, Massachusetts

Preface

Many years ago, my father's sister was diagnosed with breast cancer. During her treatments, her doctors asked if she would allow them to send some of her blood to a private lab to expand breast cancer research, specifically regarding gene mutations. Several years after she recovered from breast cancer, researchers identified that she had a newly discovered, rare genetic mutation known as CHEK2 (Checkpoint Kinase 2). Anyone with the CHEK2 gene has an increased risk of developing many different types of cancer. What was the most powerful and the most personal was that CHEK2 is a family disease. Children of a parent who has the gene have a 50/50 chance themselves of carrying the gene mutation. My father was tested, and like his sister, he had the CHEK2 gene mutation. Two of my siblings chose not to get tested and three of us did. Two of us found out that we have the gene. I am one of those two.

This genetic predisposition set the stage for my dream: to be brave enough to share my own "in-the-trenches" professional and personal hard times. My hope is that by exposing my vulnerabilities, I will be able to inspire and empower others to gain the necessary traction to jump-start their own life-changing efforts. I have always had a fascination with learning and understanding patterns of achievement. My curiosity has allowed me to absorb knowledge nuggets from the most extreme of experiences to the most joyous of occasions. I enjoy novelty and challenge in a way that expands my capacity. Sharing this wisdom has had a profound impact on my life and those within my sphere of influence. Change starts with a refreshed understanding and approach to leadership: to expand our reach to create a more positive collaborative impact and ripple effect for the greater good of our world culture.

My career goal is to foster both seasoned and emerging leaders to stretch their skills and expand their overall awareness to effect essential change. It is about energizing action towards a higher level of thought, behavior, and agility. It is also about helping leaders to adopt a philosophy of active listening, creation, inspiration, and empowerment, all of which are vitally important to build cultures of trust and collaboration.

There is great benefit in remaining curious, expanding insight, and acting on that wisdom. Our society is one of fast pace. As a C-suite trusted advisor, I find that few people truly think about their beliefs, how they are perceived, and what they would ultimately like to achieve. It has taken me decades to have that "a-ha moment" when I realized what I unquestionably wanted. Having an opportunity to inspire, coach, advise, and mentor others to reach their next level of success creates a surge of energy and excitement inside of me that is truly magical. I have found my purpose, I love what I do, and I want the same for you! Life is too short to be working at a dead-end job or settling for less than what you really want. We are all a work in progress. We are more than capable of accomplishing what we think we can only imagine – I have experienced this firsthand myself and seen it happen with others as well. We have the right to manifest feelings of triumph, joy, and satisfaction. You are the leader of your life; where your life takes you is totally up to you. Make your dreams a reality!

Introduction

In today's unprecedented environment, conventional leadership cannot take us into the future. We need to find new approaches if we aspire to dramatically increase our supply of self-aware agents of change. It is the design of *Open Your Eyes and* LEAD to offer us ways to embrace a change in leadership style that will undoubtedly impact us in every aspect of our lives.

Open Your Eyes and LEAD cuts through the roles that we find ourselves in every day and offers us powerful tools to expand our frame of reference so that we can effectively balance the art and science of leadership.

Each of us is capable of leading because each of us has the capacity to evolve. People who are intentional about their direction can emerge successfully even when life escalates. Leadership, at its core, is about empowering ourselves and those around us to face challenges and to achieve results, even with setbacks. The trajectory of leadership has been stifled due to the rapid changes and resulting pressures of our modern world.

As demands on our society expedite, the overall quality of leadership in our world is being impaired. Profit drives business. Leaders require quicker, better, faster, and cheaper results, so they are pinching wherever possible. Some leaders have lost their moral bearings. When we are rushed for results, we tend to skim-coat our actions leading to diluted and often compromised results.

Leaders who model integrity, excellence, fortitude, and kindness consistently create value and secure the biggest impact. Putting more emphasis on creating a positive and supportive culture allows for increased creativity, collaboration, and productivity. As leaders, our most valuable asset is our employees. It is imperative that we invest in them. When people's minds are excited, motivated, and engaged in what they do, the ripple effect is a catalyst, energized for triumph.

We need an upgraded leadership model to amplify progress. *Open Your Eyes and* LEAD shows readers how to become a positive force in the world by learning how to balance and then master the omnipresent tensions as we strive for leadership excellence – creating smarter decisions with better precision.

Open Your Eyes and LEAD, though not a scholarly treatise, argues that leadership is not just in our chosen field; leadership is a way of life with a calling that goes far beyond how we manage our employees. Personal leadership truly pushes the envelope because it is about utilizing our aptitude to finesse our life's vision. This image involves meaning, crafting, and taking control, with intentional direction, of what is most important to us. It is a navigation system that we create to fulfill our personal and professional aspirations.

Investing more in shaping a positive culture allows for increased collaboration, creativity, and efficiency. When people are excited, motivated, and engaged in what they do, it results in a chain reaction of more favorable outcomes. It is up to all of us to magnify our thinking. To create a permanent change in world leadership whether it be in business, academia, government, health care, or any other part of our society, we must become people-centric. We, the people, are our most valuable asset.

CHAPTER 1

Leadership

The increasingly global nature of our society requires interdependent innovative change. The common thread that cuts across all aspects of our world is leadership. Most of us think of leadership as how we manage others when we are at work, but leadership is not wholly work-centric: it is correspondingly life-centric. It is not just in our chosen field: leadership is a way of life. Personal leadership is about taking responsibility for all aspects of our lives with a positive and inspiring impact on others. Leadership is part of our human life cycle. It is in the fabric of who we are. Leaders impact every facet of our lives. We all possess some leadership capacity, and our development progresses from childhood into our advanced years if we are open to it. We are all leaders of our own lives, and it is our own unique journey that places us at various degrees of the leadership spectrum. If we look closely, unassuming leaders are all around us. This capability is formed as we encounter the opportunities and challenges of our everyday lives, traditionally measured by our successes and failures.

Our world is starving for leaders whose foundation is one of principle; whose primary objective is to build honest relationships in all aspects of their lives. Our beliefs and our conduct are often tested by external demands or strong influences from others to adjust our decisions and our actions. More than ever, the world needs leaders who can hold true to their values when life escalates, and yet it has never been tougher to be a leader… or easier to mentally and morally check out. In workplaces across the globe, people are being asked to deliver results at breakneck speed. However, when there is an overflowing necessity to produce, we tend to dilute our activity, leading to lower-quality efforts and mediocre outcomes. Those who are perpetually involved in fast and high-pressure situations feel tired and stressed, and become unengaged or disengaged. Some even jeopardize their values by taking the low road instead of the high road, just to get ahead or stay ahead. These "leaders" bring into being several shortfalls, often creating disastrous results in business and society. In the short term they may "get the job done"; however, the aftermath is destructive and creates a cultural deficit. We see this played out when people rack themselves over what is right versus what is easy. We know that seeking the path of least resistance is easier, but not always best.

There is an integrity issue with gaining wealth and success by preying upon other people's tears, fears, and anguish. This aggressive style has numerous harmful side effects, which are often overlooked due to greed. The penetrating effects of hostility exacerbate our levels of stress and unhappiness. These destructive behaviors show up in various combative ways with direct actions taking the form of being argumentative, harassing, discriminatory, or bullying, or even resorting to physical violence.

A few years ago, a client of mine was responsible for coordinating a team-building event to be attended by over 150 employees. Despite extremely inclement weather, she and a few other senior leaders came up with a creative option to keep the outdoor activities in progress. This meant that the leadership team would need to take turns being outdoors in the unpleasant weather so that they could facilitate the games. A few rogue supervisors decided that they were going to enjoy the day instead of working the event as the rest of leaders had resigned themselves to do. Instead, they developed their own rules of the game. Unbeknownst to my client, they had determined that they would place bets on their football throwing accuracy by making my client's head the new target. She was blindsided without any warning. The leader of the bullying pack had exceptional aim. His jet-propelled throw was a bullseye – a bell-ringer. The impact was quick and forceful. My client felt a strong pressure on the side of her head, followed by immediate pain. It wasn't until she was able to drag herself up from the muddy ground and had regained her focus that she realized what had happened. She heard them laughing before she saw the leader high-fiving it with his boys. He was celebrating by bragging about his accuracy and how he had won the bet. My client, on the other hand, was injured, humiliated, and disrespected.

Thankfully, she has always been gifted with the ability to think fast and talk smart. In the heat of that moment, her immediate thought was that she wanted to go straight for his jugular vein. Through our work together, she knew that wasn't the right choice, even though her next thought was how great it would feel to humiliate all of them by providing several obscenities that could have easily rolled off of her tongue. It was in that next instant that she realized that there were over 100 sets of eyes looking at her.

What we say and how we do things in the heat of the moment are influential and essential. My client had a choice to lash out at him with everything that she had in her, or she could choose to turn on a dime and shift her approach. She intensely locked eyes with the leader of this bad behavior and that was all that needed to take place. It took a tremendous amount of emotional strength to take the high road; it was not what she wanted to do, but it was what she needed to do. The most effective comeback strategy for diffusing adult bullies is to not give them the attention they are starving for. Setting the standard for how we respond when a situation compromises our dignity is far from pleasurable. After the intense staredown, she wanted it to be clear to everyone who was present that she was not afraid. Shortly after the incident, my client was informed that the leader of the gang was harshly reprimanded and his career at that company was limited from that moment forward. Even though he couldn't take back the harm he had inflicted, he was forced to apologize to her. When it comes to bullies, it is not about the specific actions, appearances, or even personalities of the victims – bullies operate to hide their own incompetence because of their own lack of self-esteem.

Many in our society glorify those with actual or perceived power or popularity. Instead, we need to refocus our mindset to honor those with stellar character traits. Core ethical values matter. Autocratic leaders who compromise their ethics and the company culture create chaos with their most valuable assets – the employees. These highly critical managers often have unrealistic expectations, rarely control their tempers, and unfailingly manage by fear; they are toxic to the company's culture. These types of hostile work environments are detrimental to the well-being of others. No one desires to work for an injurious leader: everyone favors a leader who is calm, in control, and capable of evaluating circumstances as they unfold.

Life is unpredictable, and changes often take place without notice. Part of our daily grind is spent dealing with life's myriad of challenges. Some challenges are small and easy to cruise through, while others are overwhelming. These trials confront us physically as well as psychologically. Nevertheless, the obstacles that we face help to define and support us so that we are able to learn more about ourselves. They help to mold us into the introspective people we were meant to be.

Effective behavior management impacts all types of relationships. When leaders are knowledgeable, observant, and focused on modeling respectful, trusting, supportive, and patient relationships coupled with clear communications, everyone wins. The most impactful leaders provide guidance to increase knowledge and optimize skill development. Positive leadership has an ability and a responsibility to inspire confidence and motivate others in an ethical way. Poor sportsmanship in leaders is abusive. It tears down self-esteem and patterns repugnant manners of conduct. Leading with fear, humiliation, or degrading and disrespectful behavior creates an extremely unhealthy environment that can last a lifetime. The critical success or failure factor of a team is its culture.

In addition to his corporate responsibilities, one of my clients had enjoyed playing lacrosse for many years and had a passion to give back by coaching at the high school level. Every year he had to deal with a rival coach who was known to be "a complete maniac." My client described episodes of immature temper tantrums and verbal assaults as common occurrences whenever they played this coach's team. The coach's demeanor towards referees was downright rude, and his aggressive posture towards opposing coaching staff was equally combative. He displayed no respect towards others, and his behavior was juvenile. His lacrosse team displayed equally poor sportsmanship when they mimicked his attitudes and behaviors. Many of his players were very sneaky and performed illegal and harmful hits after the play was over. It was commonplace for his players to utter obscenities not just towards the players on other teams, but towards the coaches and officials as well. His formative players adopted the abrasive style and behaviors that they were exposed to by their coach. This arrogant team was known as a bunch of "entitled punks," creating bad blood and resentment throughout the league. This team's culture continued to deteriorate, which fostered reputational damage both for the school and for the town. This leader destroyed morale by demeaning everyone around him, including his own players. For numerous seasons, this bully-styled coach put many athletes' confidence, focus, self-esteem, motivation, and overall enjoyment of life both in and out of the sport at risk. The strong influence of these types of tyrannizing actions on student athletes creates a wave of bad habits and negative actions towards others that is frequently unleashed for the rest of their lives.

The browbeating and mistreating of these young athletes eventually led to the coach being released from his position.

This story isn't solely about lacrosse: this story is about how we behave as leaders when we find ourselves in competitive situations. Competition is beneficial if it doesn't veer into the space of unethical or disrespectful behavior. We all have people in our lives who are influenced by our actions, so being aware of and having appreciation for those who are seeking cues from our conduct is critical. We always want to set the right example rather than demonstrate a destructive demeanor.

In the entry for "leadership," the thesaurus lists words such as: to control, command, rule, sway, dominate, supreme, power, and superiority. These words relate to an old leadership style where organizations had a more straightforward hierarchy and role authority was considered enough for a leader to motivate others. With many different generations in our workforce, the leadership styles of the past need to be transformed.

Those in a position of decision-making should be basing their choices on facts, awareness, understanding, and carefully intended judgments versus random choices on a personal whim. Arbitrary leadership promotes deceptive environments that are often flooded with tendencies of faking, hiding, and lying. These leaders spend unproductive time and energy steering other people's impressions of them so that only their favorable side is shown. They play politics to hide their deficiencies, uncertainties, and limitations.

The word "leadership" should be about the capability to adapt to and spearhead any situation with integrity. At the same time, it should also be about the ability to create and clearly communicate a vision or a new direction by inspiring, empowering, developing, and motivating people to engage and to achieve more. In my experience, highly skilled, well-respected leaders use the same authentic decision-making methodology whether it is to have an impact on their personal life, their professional life, or both. Their motives and choices remain consistent whether the resolution impacts only them, or it affects the lives of others as well. This strategy holds true even when the upshot is in the height of critical times.

Culture comes from within, and it is up to the leadership to create the right environment. As leaders, we should have a thought pattern of helping people to be their natural best. Crafting and implementing a sustainable agenda that boosts energy, morale, and productivity will serve to encourage, expand, and strengthen returns.

The best-of-the-best in leadership have a curious thirst for knowledge and capitalize on the opportunity to hydrate every day. No one is immune to tough luck or poor choices. The crème de la crème leaders learn early on to rely upon trusted advisors. These guiding partners build a bond over time by sharing unique and deep insights that will best support their clients. This closely linked and confidential relationship provides constructive counsel on sensitive matters, complex challenges, and major decisions. An external trusted advisor provides unique value. Many of the leader's problems, hopes, and fears cannot be deliberated with internal people because these matters must be kept close to the vest.

Over the past 30 years, I have interacted with many leaders. Those who were the most successful were those who had dealt with and overcome substantial adversity at some point in their lives. Growing stronger through intense situations enables powerful skills to emerge that will support leaders in all aspects of their future if leveraged appropriately. These transferable skills are the common denominator that most favorably impacts the best leaders to achieve extraordinary results. These leaders have the wherewithal to own their actions while still growing from any and all setbacks.

Great leaders also possess conceptual abilities, critical thinking, and problem-solving skills that, when combined with their adaptive abilities, can predicate success. Possessing these core competencies denotes leaders in both our personal and professional lives. Highly adept leaders infuse themselves and those around them with positive energy and a clear vision, sparking the kind of enthusiasm that encourages and empowers favorable results.

When our team members know that they can rely upon us for sound decisions, they will follow our lead through thick and thin. When our character is one of dependability, it provides comfort to others, especially during times of change.

Those leaders who are truly committed to progress have their eyes wide open to the engagement level of their teams. The emotional and behavioral connection at work is more important than ever before. Tangible rewards like benefits and perks, the demands required for their specific role, and opportunities that the business offers them, are all top priorities to consistently stay abreast of in an effort to maximize retainment of key contributors. Leaders should be focused on empowering their employees and holding them accountable, while shaping and supporting their growth and development. This results in our most valuable assets feeling empowered, engaged, and energized. Leading high-performing teams requires curating a customized, individualized approach. Employees need different levels of mentoring, training, motivation, feedback, and support to reach their full potential. As leaders, we should be gaining a better understanding of what each of our employees' natural aptitudes are, and then looking for opportunities to support them in expanding upon their unique talents. This also includes understanding how each person thinks, feels, and behaves: the true fabric of who they are. When leadership focuses on positioning people to use their best skills to do their best work, everyone benefits. This style of actionable leadership optimizes employees' talents, and improves performance, overall productivity, and results. This commitment to excellence increases team dynamics. When we like what we do, we regenerate our own energy to overcome obstacles and produce higher-quality outcomes.

None of us has a crystal ball to know what the emerging business realities will be, nor how employees will respond to these shifts. These are disruptive, conflicting, and very complex issues. Exceptional leadership is more important than ever before. The accelerated pace of change will require leaders to stay nimble and adapt quickly to innovative workplace management strategies. The prosperity of our future depends on leaders emerging with thoughts, attitudes, and behaviors that can respond to the rising speed of change with impactful and innovative solutions.

Leadership excellence does not mean we try to please everyone. That is impossible. Our focus should be on treating people, in all aspects of our life, with fairness, respect, and kindness. The majority of people will recognize and appreciate that. Exemplary leaders have a great deal of patience and mental fortitude. Developing the strength and ability to get through adversity by executing effective solutions and coming out the other side with the desired results is very beneficial and so desperately needed for our future.

Great leaders are vastly skilled communicators. They forge their connections through a deep understanding of other people and an astute ability to speak directly to their wants and needs. They are truly generous and regularly offer enthusiastic accolades. Nurturing relationships where there is influence-with-integrity affects the thoughts and actions of others. Leaders who are as committed to the achievement of other people's aspirations as they are to their own successes are higher-regarded leaders. When we genuinely care and celebrate the accomplishments of others, we inspire others in an authentic way.

Inspiring and guiding others is a critical factor in leadership. How we each react to and handle the "bumpiness" of our world is being observed by others. Refresh your enthusiasm and intentionality to lead by example. Consistently going the extra distance for others will often give rise to them going the extra mile for you.

Those who can set the pace to innovate, organize, motivate, and influence others create a beneficial ripple effect of future progress. This ambiance of camaraderie has a huge benefit for collaboration, motivating employees to strive for excellence. A leader's ethical fibers earn respect and instill positive energy to support the team in delivering the peak amount of quality work possible even during highly stressful situations.

In addition to an ethical mindset, emotional intelligence is a critical skill that all leaders need to develop if they desire to empower change and record sustainable achievements. Emotional intelligence is the capacity to accurately recognize, interpret, and guide emotions within ourselves and others to expedite thinking. Emotional competencies have a significant impact on performance and attitude, allowing for ease of relationship building, which impacts social cohesion. This mediating role inspires innovation and growth, while encouraging teams to leverage the unique strengths and contributions of each member.

Admirable leaders also possess a reputable character. Conduct is mainly determined by values and holds true for every area in our lives. The resolve to stay genuine, also referred to as being our authentic selves, is based upon what we believe to be the right direction even when nobody's watching. Those leaders who embrace the art of listening with compassion are in a much better position to be successful in our increasingly multigenerational workforce. When employees say they want their voices to be heard, they are saying that they want leaders who will not just hear them, but who will actively and empathetically listen to them. Empathy is a powerful display of comprehension. Many of us avoid emotional interactions, especially in business. The best leaders know how to empathize and make themselves approachable to those who may need special consideration. Great leaders invest in activities that balance the head and the heart to create meaningful relationships. Employees aren't just tools and resources provided for the leader's success: they bring a wealth of unique capabilities and aptitudes. Leaders who care about their employees' well-being build performance, relationships, and influential currency. To improve meaningful relationships and organizational possibilities, leaders need to think longer and harder about employee satisfaction. People tend to work harder and aim to exceed expectations when they feel that they are genuinely cared about. Those leaders who remain authentic to their moral core principles naturally gain and retain more credibility.

The reality is that our workplaces are fluid and rapidly evolving. This shift in the workforce requires a new leadership style with unconventional ideas. In addition to creating and sustaining an agile workplace, the need for meaningful, collaborative work is very attractive to today's workforce. This approach increases profitability, performance, engagement, and retention of the employees and the customers. Those who are new in our workforce won't stay with their employers for the length of time that prior generational workforces traditionally did. The future of the workplace will be markedly different because of the rapid advances in technology, and the different needs, wants, and views of the upcoming generations.

Currently, I believe there is an erosion in our world's potential due to a significant lack of focus on leadership development specifically around inspiration, character, and culture. It is time to cultivate leadership in an intentional and thoughtful way for the betterment of the generations to come. As a society, we must escalate our efforts to establish an increased number of leadership teams who have been trained specifically to support the goals and objectives of today. This augmentation will create a vibrant pipeline of emerging leaders who will be better prepared for the unknowns of the future. Those who expand their "intellectual muscles" can show up by providing value and contribute a treasured blend that is especially beneficial in our ever-changing, fast-paced world.

Top Nuggets of Wisdom

1 The common thread that cuts across all aspects of our world is leadership – we need to be intentional in leading our own lives, personally and professionally.

2 Our world is starving for leaders with more integrity.

3 There are specific character traits that distinguish effective leaders from "bad" leaders.

CHAPTER 2

Bold Moves

Bold moves require disrupting the status quo. They are often radical strategic changes. Breakthroughs happen when we are open to reframing the ways of the past. Revolutionary change is about doing what others are afraid of or haven't even thought about doing. Rapid change is often more successful than gradual change because it gives rise to a deeper focus of energy. Doing your best will allow you to become your best. Those with a deep inner conviction, coupled with the courage for action, make bold moves a reality.

An existing CEO client of mine hired a new vice president of sales. The company was in the middle of a rapid growth period, and all hands were on deck with a major technology launch. The CEO asked if I could support it by working with its newest senior leader to get her up to speed as efficiently and effectively as possible. This was not part of my traditional work, but my client's business was in a period of accelerated expansion. I was well seasoned with the company and well positioned to ramp her up quickly. During one of our first casual conversations, she shared with me what had become her epiphany: she finally realized that she wanted, needed, and deserved a completely new life. She had been miserable in her marriage for years. Her husband had been laid off over ten years earlier, but he had been unwilling or unable to gain employment since that time. Instead, he had used and abused her, as is the case in so many domestic abuse scenarios, and she had tolerated it. When she finally decided that enough was enough, she took the necessary steps to get divorced. She gained custody of their two children and she relocated with them to a new state. She bought a new home and then started this new job, all within a very short window of time. She refreshed her allegiances. Her passion and her courageous actions were fueled by wanting more out of life for herself and her children. These dramatic shifts in her life were very tough and equally frightening, but she believed that if she wanted more out of life then she needed to gather up the resolution to make it happen; she did just that. Her deep inner conviction for a better life was extremely difficult. Her bold moves displayed her transferable courageous leadership skills to support her in her personal life as well as in her professional advancements. She was a stellar leader because she had a vision that allowed her to take a huge shot in the dark with her eyes wide open.

We are as courageous as we think we are. Pessimistic thoughts create defeatist outcomes. When we exude a bad attitude, we are failing before we even begin. While concentrating on the good in our universe is not always easy, it encourages optimistic thinking which allows for more productive after-effects. Those of us who have a brighter outlook on life are more apt to regularly establish attainable goals.

We will all face adversity. Part of growing and learning is to endure hardships. Whether we like it or not, life is full of constant changes that can shake up our world. Our baseline when dealing with adversity starts from our own unparalleled place. Our desires and approaches differ, which is why we vary in how we each react to unfavorable fortune or fate. Those who survive the best, and who are even capable of thriving, are the ones who are able to interpret and rapidly adapt to the new state of affairs. They center their attention on examining and determining the problems and then taking systematic action posthaste.

What goes without saying is that those who have the courage to make bold moves usually face more hard knocks than those who play it safe. Bold moves are also a big part of how and why dreams come true. The essence of being a great leader is being able to bounce back both smarter and stronger from adversity. Mental toughness, or "grit" as it is often referred to, adds more distinction than a person's intellect or talent does. Intellectual endurance is about controlling our thoughts, behaviors, and emotions during demanding times. It takes more than just aptitude to reach our goals: it is our beliefs, our perspectives, and our focus, combined with the passion to excel, that create our attitude and aptitude. It is important for leaders to stay focused on caring about the people, the process, and the results. Those who can balance their passion with beneficial human interactions inspire others to follow their lead. Those who can expand their mental robustness gain more fortitude and clarity to take calculated leaps of faith to venture into the unknown. Acquiring that risk-taking spirit and grit is what helps to challenge the status quo.

I coached a young academician whose career trajectory could be compared to a bolt of lightning. She was focused, curious, and committed. She was determined, and she worked diligently every day. While still under the age of 30, she was promoted very quickly from adjunct faculty, to full-time faculty, to associate dean, to dean of faculty, all within less than five years. She told everyone in her world that she had found her dream job.

About two years into her employment, things started to change dramatically. Benefits that had once been tried and true were being taken away with little or no notice. Long-standing employees were being laid off. Gender discrimination seemed to be in the air as fewer female employees were part of the rank and file.

While she was known by everyone, from students to faculty, to be the superstar at this university, she still hadn't had decades of life experience to draw from when these tough times arrived. What added years to her life experience was the coaching work that we did together. We had already talked about and worked on expanding and mastering her mental toughness. Individual resilience is based on survival skills from past experiences. Grit can be found even in our newer leaders.

Embodying grit to her meant that she didn't have to compromise her leadership style to conform to the behaviors that she had not only been witnessing, but also been experiencing on a regular basis. Instead, she took control of her career and found her voice. This meant that she displayed bravery by requesting meetings with key members of the administration. She stayed true to her values with both her words and her actions by trying to bring awareness and then fix the challenges she was observing. She was seeing the morale within the university plummet, which was hard for her to watch. Her mental toughness allowed her to comment not only on the gender discrimination issues, but also on the racist viewpoints that were becoming part of the administration's culture. Unfortunately, her passion to right these wrongs fell on deaf ears.

She had put forth her best effort but was still incapable of making the necessary impact. She had to accept what she could not change. Though the toxic extenuating circumstances elevated the need for her to walk away from her once dream job, her commitment to be true to herself allowed her to come up with a "Plan B" for her career. Her resignation allowed her to then transition to a new role in academia with new goals and a genuine excitement for her future.

We have the ability to create change. Dramatic adjustments often come from making courageous decisions. Sometimes it is forced upon us, while other times we are intentional about taking a less than conventional path. Whether it is in our personal world or in business, we need to move away from our current state of affairs in order to grow. Bold moves often happen when we are standing at the intersection of major unhappiness or pain and we have to take a leap of faith if our ultimate goal is a better future. Varying levels of fear go hand-in-hand with transition. We can squash fear by stepping outside of our comfort zone over and over again until the discomfort starts to feel more like the norm. With time, training, and a desire to change, courage can be learned and achieved.

To be most effective when contemplating a bold move, we must allow ourselves to optimize our boundaries while simultaneously calculating our risks and uncertainties. We all have different levels of expectations and tolerance when it comes to risk and return. Therefore, the risk/reward curve needs to be carefully deliberated for realistic and endurable expectations.

A venture capitalist client of mine was interested in providing private equity for a potential high-growth manufacturing company. Statistically, failure rates for venture capitalist investments are high, which is why she obtained my services. We, along with many others, collaborated on the essential due diligence process, which was rigorous and complicated. I was focused on both grounding my client's expectations in reality, to make sure her interest was a worthwhile investment, and ascertaining whether this venture was fast-growing enough for a healthy return on her investment. Oftentimes, with these types of business deals, there is a lack of effectiveness in communication which leads to many business deals failing. By aligning their goals and objectives, and establishing frequent meetings, we were able to mitigate a number of disastrous situations. My client eventually provided the initial seed funding and was the primary financial backer for this start-up. A critical part of my work with this client was to prime her to go into the business deal with her eyes wide open, especially to the high risk that she would be assuming. When investors participate in smaller and early-stage companies, they usually gain significant control over the company and its decisions, in addition to a significant portion of the company's ownership with the hopes of consequential value. The founders had a great deal of experience in this industry. Between the owner and the venture capitalist, we felt that they had a solid opportunity for success. The initial investment was sizable. Over time, it became even more financially demanding due to the ramp-up of the business being delayed for a variety of unexpected and complex reasons. The financial burn rate was crushing. The uncertainties were mammoth. People often underestimate the length of time, the effort, and the amount of money it takes to launch and gain momentum with a new business. The pressures, obstacles, and time constraints were extreme, causing regular and severe strain between the founder and my client. In spite of the constant hardship, they were able to stay true to their character and persevere. There were many occasions when my client was second-guessing whether this venture would eventually pay off. During those stormy times, I encouraged her to keep pushing things forward because it was apparent to me that there was a solid foundation emerging. Ironically, just at the time when conditions appeared to be falling apart, they were actually falling right into place. As an external viewer, I could see that deliberate progress had been made towards success.

Sadly, for all of us, their short-sighted business decision led the venture capitalist to terminate my services as a way to save money. Unfortunately, they were so deeply entrenched in the day-to-day difficulties, the founder and my client had lost the collaborative energy and effective communication that they had once shared. They were too submerged in the problems to see that they were on the cusp of triumph. Within less than six months of my departure, they were looking to dissolve the business. They simply ran out of steam due to their rapid growth pains and the intense financial strain. The irony was that they were not able to stand back and observe that the heavy lifting to build the business had already been accomplished.

When we find ourselves in a highly demanding space of time, it is helpful to be introspective; to openly and honestly assess our circumstances. If we summon the audacity and the perseverance to stretch outside of our comfort zone for a bit longer than we think we can, we will experience a burst of freedom that will kindle amazing shifts in our destiny. It is not easy, but it is possible to thrive through adversity if we stay the course. Making bold moves through calculated risk-taking is vital in stimulating change.

Top Nuggets of Wisdom

1 Making bold moves does not guarantee success.

2 We all face adversity. Those who focus on a brighter yet realistic outlook are more apt to regularly attain their goals.

3 There are certain essential character traits, both personal and professional, for success in accomplishing bold moves.

CHAPTER 3

Trailblazers

Since the beginning of human history, pioneers have navigated the course of uncharted territories. They are risk takers who draw upon leaps of faith by following the path they believe is predestined for them.

When we have the right intentions and we follow our passion, everything else will follow. Throughout history, innovation and perseverance have been vital for achievement. From a young age, we learned about the courageous men and women who left their steadfast lives behind to explore and then to settle new lands. We also learned about innovative people who spearheaded an ingenious technique, a new area of knowledge, or an exciting venture, or who advanced an activity. While we may not consider ourselves to be part of an elite group, we can each add value to this universe in our own special way if we choose to.

Trailblazers have a passion to build a better world. They have a vision for a brighter future. They are determined to cut through even the most difficult of barriers. These resourceful innovators take the lead and the risks by pointing others in the best direction forward. The most successful trailblazers incorporate the ability to learn from their failures and setbacks. This grants them the growth opportunities to evolve their unique qualities of emotional and physical strength, as well as their courage. It empowers them with the ability to be even more unyielding in their quest for innovation.

Sometimes, we are intentional about trailblazing, and other times there is a radical disruption in our life that causes the pioneer within us to come alive and wake us up to the fact that we actually are a trailblazer.

My childhood was plagued with a life-threatening combination of severe allergies and acute asthma. In the early 1960s, medical breakthroughs were not as prevalent as they are today, so children with this dire blend often didn't survive. I often fell asleep when the academic basics were taught due to the side effects of the powerful medications that I needed to take. First grade was especially difficult because I was both verbally and physically abused by my teacher, who was also a nun. She slapped my knuckles with a ruler, slammed my head against the blackboard, and grabbed my cheeks and squeezed them while simultaneously pummeling my head from side to side. With the traumatic behavior I was subjected to by my teacher, combined with being sick on an ongoing basis, it was difficult for me to learn. My grades in my first year of school produced many Ds and a few Fs.

The silver lining for me was that my mother was my biggest advocate, and she was on a mission. She learned that the state that we lived in had recently voted to provide services to all students, not just to those who attended public school. Her one-woman campaign was centered around calling the Department of Education non-stop. She left message after message, but they never called her back. Eventually, someone picked up the telephone at the Department of Education and gave in to her nuisance calls. Her persistence paid off when I was able to receive special tutoring at the parochial school that I was attending. Not only was I the first, but I was also the only student to receive these services. The tutoring continued until I had attained my grade level. To complement the tutoring, my mother found a summer school program for students who needed extra academic support. This was also the guarantee that there would be no interruption in my learning.

The luminaries of our world are inspired by something deep within them to do something creative. Their catalyst may be a dream, a desire, or a vision. These pioneering leaders challenge the status quo. They create a renewed sense of purpose and a shared concept, which makes a difference in their overall accomplishments. That capacity, infused with the relentless drive for excellence, inspires and creates enduring success.

Decades later, while moving through my own journey of self-discovery, I was finally able to comprehend the priceless gift that my mother had shared with me: she had given me a roadmap to become a trailblazer in my own life. Whether we are advocating for a sick child like my mother did, or going full steam ahead to start a new venture, trailblazers are a special breed who are ready to accelerate their results. They can allow their imagination to be their guide in creating new possibilities with better outcomes. You don't need to follow someone else's path: you have what it takes inside of you to choose to find the road less traveled. To get the results that are most important to you, target the possibilities that come with each new day.

Leaders in the 21st century are expected to navigate innovative realms in business. Human potential, performance, and drive vary for everyone. We are each unique in our personalities, abilities, experiences, strengths, weaknesses, and morals. Our distinctive constellation of attributes expands possibilities when utilized to bring about positive transformation. Groundbreaking leaders courageously leave behind the known for the potential of what could be. This expedition into the unknown necessitates a vision, wisdom, conviction, tenacity, and a sense of adventure. Just like we use a GPS to get us from point A to point B, we need trailblazers in business who can be our navigation system – whether it is calculating our current position, providing the best direction forward, keeping track of the speed of progress, or charting the time to the new destination. These pioneers will best support us as we transition into our new world of commerce.

I worked with a client who was a registered nurse who also had a master's degree in Public Health. For many years, she had witnessed patients unnecessarily suffer because traditional medical professionals either were not aware, did not understand, or were unwilling to support alternative ways of healing beyond western medicine. She knew that modern medicine needed to be linked with proven practices from other healing traditions to relieve the medical, physical, emotional, social, spiritual, and environmental influences that can affect a person's health and well-being. She was confident that it was time for a transformational shift in how medical care was being delivered, and she was determined to be that catalyst.

Integrative medicine is a blend of modern "scientific" medicine with authenticated alternative methods from around the world. It focuses on the importance of the medical practitioner viewing the patient as a whole person, with a commitment to using all suitable therapeutic methods to attain optimal health and healing.

As a trusted advisor, I helped her to process through "what was keeping her up at night" so that she could gain clarity about what she was most passionate about. She found great value in collaborating and strategizing a variety of different perspectives to determine what were the most efficient and effective paths forward for her business. Together, we uncovered her "blind spots," allowing her to expand her reach to gain awareness in areas that she had not had experience in prior to our work together. She became a force to be reckoned with: a catalyst for a worldwide movement to communicate fact-based research that would bring greater awareness and validity to additional techniques for healing.

She knew that her vision would need additional high-level medical experts, so she started her company by leveraging her Rolodex of collaborative relationships with Ph.D.s, M.D.s, and other medical professionals. Her dream was to publish new evidence-based research that would expand awareness of alternative, but viable, approaches to providing quality care that would promote healing on all levels. My client and her team spent countless hours creating the publication's platform. She maintained rigorous standards for herself, her team, and the publication.

Because of the great divide between eastern and western medicine, she underestimated the timeline for how complicated it would be to promote a broader collaboration between all of the stakeholders. It took her more than six years to make her vision a reality. Her multimedia publishing platform now provides a voice for cutting-edge clinical, educational, and policy advances for the benefit of academic establishments and healthcare organizations worldwide. Her consistent audacious endeavors allowed for sophisticated medical intellectuals to have a platform to share their findings in a communication vehicle that is now available in multiple languages in more than 40 countries.

Leaders who style themselves as frontrunners who others want to follow are bona fide trailblazers whose impact is inarguable. They enhance their lives and those around them by being specific and intentional about their choices. They build a foundation for success by expanding benchmarks of achievement via clear communications. They then walk-the-talk with exemplary character, honesty, positive energy, and a vision that includes the necessary steps to inspire impressive change.

A "brilliant mind" at a top-ranked private research university is at the frontier of controlling diseases. This principal investigator has a lifelong quest to make a difference in our world by continuing to expand his teaching and research to save lives. His groundbreaking efforts of achievement fill an important gap and extend the range of possibilities.

This professor's state-of-the art laboratory and his team of researchers had been making well-respected, internationally recognized progress. His passion for transformative developments within his area of specialty was being interrupted by escalated human dynamics challenges with a few colleagues within his immediate academic community. He was referred to me by a mutual business acquaintance.

Starting from "Hello," I could sense that he was beyond frustrated with his inability to handle the elevated human dynamics issues which placed him well outside of his comfort zone. He was being exposed to sniping from administrators as well as from some of his peers. There was criticism of his teaching ability being made through backchannels and then delivered to him either second hand or not at all. The pushback, politics, and lack of support were unquestionable. He explained to me that the pressure to perform, to publish, and to win research grants was intense, with the stakes and consequences being colossal. He is a trailblazer with his high-impact teaching, research, and regular international speaking engagements. Scholars of his caliber should be viewed as a valuable asset instead of as a threat. Extreme competition often breeds toxic environments. With this type of fierce pressure, there will inevitably be those individuals who will play dirty politics, especially when it involves either cutting-edge research, securing intellectual properties, gaining funding, or intellectual independence. It is difficult to find the proper balance between the critical roles of research and education for faculty members at research universities. To keep our world evolving, innovation is critically needed. Our global society greatly benefits from and depends upon these research enterprises.

Our potent work together continues as I support and guide him on how best to navigate this culture-clash environment. He lives in a world full of scholars who should be collegial, but in his professional life he finds himself stepping around and over landmines. Our collaborative efforts are focused on covering his blind spots and supporting him to pick up the pace of prodigious traction on his lifelong quest of being a catalytic force for scaling breakthrough research. His passion is deep-rooted to alter the course of debilitating diseases. He has the intellectual capacity to save and improve millions of lives. However, if he can't learn to dovetail his approach with the present system, his self-esteem will have been irreparably compromised and his brilliance will have been for naught.

Trailblazers, like all of us, can fail. Failure is a form of knowledge and knowledge is power. Groundbreakers set themselves apart from the average person because they have learned the requisite skills and are determined to dust themselves off and try, try again. They have mastered the art of "failing better" by extracting value from their mistakes. In order to keep ingenuity on the upswing, we need to remain dynamic and nimble; to flex in the best way possible as circumstances present themselves. To increase the trajectory of your life, be constructive with your intentions and your attitudes. To model the trendsetters in our world takes hard work, consistency, dedication, and a strong desire to achieve.

Top Nuggets of Wisdom

1 Trailblazers have existed since the beginning of time.

2 Pioneers enhance their lives and the lives of those around them by being specific and intentional about their choices.

3 Failure is a form of knowledge and knowledge advances our aptitude. Successful trailblazers master the art of "failing better."

CHAPTER 4

Stretch

Opportunities in life are not equally distributed. Talent alone doesn't get us very far. To achieve, we need to keep trying our very hardest when we are confronted with criticism, opposition, or unfavorable circumstances. Even when we feel beaten down and tired, we need to be constantly pushing ourselves if we want to succeed. This requires stretching beyond our elasticity of comfort. To truly find ourselves, we need to think, act, and react for ourselves alone. Combining what we see with what we know to be our truth will expand our mental capacity, maturity, and character.

There are many elements to leadership. Setting out the right life trajectory provides for more long-term advancement. This can only happen when we are genuine and know ourselves well. There is comfort in knowing our sweet spot. Once we are to develop and own our uniqueness, we can then show up as our true self every day. When we are able to clearly articulate what we like and what we don't, what we are good at and what we aren't, we can then differentiate ourselves from others. Understanding our unique skills and abilities is valuable if we desire to grasp and then acknowledge our very own secret ingredients. Look to be more intentional on a regular basis. Remain on the path of seeking out opportunities that resonate with your personal values, your vision, your goals, and your strengths.

Several years ago, two married couples combined their resources and their experience to purchase an established business. From the outset, all four of them put a great deal of effort into increasing revenue while also significantly improving the business processes and the quality of work life for their employees. They accomplished this by re-engineering many of the outdated and inefficient policies and procedures so that the business would be able to thrive. The investment paid off and the business flourished. Their dreams had come true. They were comfortable with their personal income, their business revenue, and the balance of personal and professional time in their lives. The well-known saying "all that glitters isn't gold" could be applied to what happened next. While my clients were happy with the great strides that had been made, they learned in due course that they had been blindsided: the other couple had been working behind the scenes to bully my clients into leaving the business. This disheartening and devastating event erupted into a hostile situation.

The true test of leadership can undoubtedly be witnessed during times of crisis. Performance under pressure is critical. A crisis like this is devastating. Over a three-year period, I worked to help them to be able to "keep their wits about them" during a time when both their personal and professional lives were completely disrupted. I kept them focused on the necessity for smart, proactive, and rapid reactive decision-making. There were times when the situation went into emergency mode, and at those times I provided 24/7 support. I helped them to defuse their stress with intentionality. We concentrated on having clear goals and expectations in order to be able to make the wisest decisions based on the information that was available at that moment. Curveballs were consistently being thrown in their direction and I was their unswerving "rock of positive support," advising them in a manner that created successful timely outcomes. The commitment to stay the course and to continue to push forward with a high degree of integrity and a positive attitude would be challenging for anyone in their situation. I remained in the trenches with them so that they could stay on track to rise above the conflict. I kept them fixated on strategic planning for the best possible future outcomes.

They felt that their entire world was falling apart. Their emotional and mental strain was at an all-time high – a state of being stretched beyond capacity. Their prior life challenges had prepared them to stretch themselves even through the most extreme of uncomfortable times. This situation was well beyond their emotional elasticity; they were about to break. Oftentimes when we are dealing with very intense situations, we narrow our attention and fold into ourselves with a gravitational pull towards inescapable doom.

I advised them to not let all of the negativity in their world give them a bad disposition. Instead, they should use that fuel to spark the fire of progress in a new direction. They needed to look at things through a different lens so that they could view the many positives in their situation. They had been stuck in a "comfortable rut" at their old company, and this antagonistic situation forced them to look for greener pastures – which they did. I asked them to visualize what they really wanted their lives to look like. They felt overwhelmed with that question, so we broke it down into more bite-size chunks. We then focused on the process of elimination. This helped us to gain a better understanding of what they *didn't* want. Once we had a better handle on that, we focused on what they referred to as the most intimidating question: what they aspired to be. We had several emotional conversations to sort out what that might look like and what their next steps would need to be towards making their "intimidating" goal a reality. I cataloged what each of them aspired to be both personally and professionally. We established that their endgame was to create a state-of-the-art manufacturing business. Through innovative thinking, they were able to dissolve the original partnership, which created the opportunity for them to stretch themselves beyond their wildest dreams – an experience of a lifetime. They were energetic and optimistic about their plan for the future. However, they didn't know what they didn't know. This happens with all of us when we venture into a new experience. Starting a business can be very risky. Large numbers of new businesses fail during the first few years. Often there is not enough demand or sustainability for the products or services. Having a good grasp of the competition's strengths and weaknesses, combined with having a clear view of your own business's points of difference, is key. Strategic planning is critically important prior to launching the company, along with maintaining and updating the plan regularly throughout the company's existence.

As ambassadors of their newly created business, my clients experienced an abundance of information overload. They found themselves overwhelmed by the many risks and challenges, along with the numerous decision-making obstacles that surfaced on a daily basis. Through our ongoing work together, I helped them to prioritize the issues that were the most pressing as well as the most significant. They took on each challenge and managed it to the best of their abilities even though they felt as if they were drinking from a fire hose. I consistently supported them in their efforts to make smart decisions with the best precision. All the while, my premeditated goal was to keep them from drowning.

They emerged stronger, more knowledgeable, more seasoned in many different aspects of business, and more calculated in their risk-taking and decision-making strategies. The icing on the cake was uncovering what they valued most, which was the strength of their marriage and the joy from their family bond.

Today, their professional careers are thriving. Finding the balance between the day-to-day tactical operations and the strategic decisions is not easy. As their careers continue to grow, they are relentless in doing their very best with both. I was ecstatic to be an integral part of helping them to transform what could have been their worst business nightmare into their brightest possible future.

We unearth and evolve different facets of ourselves through experiences. When we blend our introspection with experimenting with our identities, it allows us to grow and find the right path forward. When we challenge ourselves to stretch beyond the zone where we sense comfort, we learn the utmost about our abilities, and it unleashes excitement for what is forthcoming.

Too many people live a life without much joy and settle for their existing circumstances. Balancing life's demands is a common human experience that can be overwhelming. Many people have substantial weight on them stemming from a variety of responsibilities and obligations that may include, but not be limited to, financial, family, employment, and community.

On occasions, it is hard to know if life is passing us by or if it is trying to run us over. Knowing that we are responsible for our own happiness, we need to be intentional about how we take care of ourselves. Setting limits to strike a more desirable balance is an ongoing process that is essential to caring for our own quality of life. Many of my clients struggle with putting themselves first. The advice that I give to my clients, and that I've adopted as well, is to strive to "give" more strategically to others, rather than to make random unconscious commitments that will be hard to fulfill. Attempt to be deliberate about where and how you spend your time, your money, and your effort. Pinpoint opportunities that directly relate to your larger purpose in life and that will have the most meaningful impact. This will allow you to have the time and energy to branch out in the way that is best for you.

At a dinner meeting of enterprising female professionals, an attorney sought me out for what I expected to be a casual conversation. She confided that she was envious of me because I was able to leave corporate America and start my own business. She desired to experience a similar excitement in her work that I felt when I was able to help others. My immediate response was to offer to support her so that she could identify the essential changes that she needed to make in her life. She shared that she was divorced and that she was raising their three kids on her own. I asked her a variety of questions that related to things that she had not thought about previously. This provided her with a platform of different options so that she could make her dream a reality just as I was able to do. As we departed from the dinner, I wished her well and told her that I was just a phone call away if she wanted to talk further.

About six months later, we found ourselves at the same professional meeting at opposite sides of a very large room. When the meeting adjourned, she immediately worked her way over to let me know that she had been thinking about me and how I had helped her to make her dream a reality! She said,

> *I kept hearing your words in my mind over and over. Your words helped me to gain the necessary strength I needed to take the requisite steps to start my own firm. I had been extremely worried that I would not have enough business to support my kids and me. I never imagined I'd be so busy right out of the gate.*

She has since hired me to support her as she expands her practice in exciting new ways.

We need more people like her who are brave, smart, and forward thinking, and who, while making proactive choices, can rally the courage and possess the inbred grit to see things through. The possibilities and opportunities are endless if you are truly committed to stretching yourself.

People change when they are ready, willing, and able to – when it becomes their highest priority. We are willing to change when we firmly decide to leave the past behind us and embark upon a new future. Sadly, many people live with regret about something in their past that they don't seem able to get beyond. We can't revise history, but we can reappraise, apologize, forgive, forget, let go, and inevitably accept what we cannot change by taking personal responsibility. This happens when we understand the disparity between our goals and our present state and autonomously choose to close that gap. It is inevitable that we will face challenges because our world consists of non-stop change. If we remain aware and understand the core of our thoughts and actions, we will be able to keep them in check towards achieving our purpose. Plans that put more energy into capitalizing on strengths instead of over-analyzing weaknesses always produce better results. The choices that we make are our own responsibility. Even the smallest of selections that we make today could have a profound impact in either a favorable or an unfavorable way for years to come. Don't allow past dilemmas to wreak havoc with your present and future. Denial and resistance can be overcome.

I was asked to address a group of CEOs about the importance of business culture. After my presentation, I had the pleasure of talking with several of the attendees. One of the participants pulled me aside to ask if I would be willing to help him on a "special project" that was near and dear to his heart. He innately knew that he needed direction from a strategic planning and implementation standpoint, but he knew that he needed to get me to "buy in" if he were to propel his "project" forward. He used his storytelling expertise to share information with me about his background. He explained that he had been raised by a single mom in a financially strapped household. He was able to survive his inner-city neighborhood because he possessed savvy street smarts. As soon as he was old enough to enlist, he was off to Vietnam. He witnessed unimaginable death and destruction due to the daily onslaught of fierce weapon fire. Day after day, he lived a nightmare by filling green body bags with bodies of his fellow Marines who had been ripped apart by projectiles and weaponry. The survivor's guilt and emotional turmoil haunted him for years because he had received the "gift of life" unlike many of his fellow Marines. Those coming home in body bags had paid the greatest price – their lives. When he had completed his tour of duty, he was adamant that he would find a way to make a difference; to never forget those who had paid that final price. His passion was to improve the quality of life for children, especially those who came from tough, underprivileged backgrounds like he had.

His thirst for knowledge spurred him to acquire a Doctorate in Philosophy from a prestigious university. He received a host of awards but it still wasn't enough for him; he was preoccupied with stretching his skills to make an even bigger impact. This former Marine was passionate about creating sustainable models of school success that would improve administrator and teacher effectiveness as evidenced by measurable student achievement goals. Additionally, he wanted to assist with the creation of school communities to support a climate and culture that would promote peace and economic prosperity throughout the world.

He started his own consulting practice, but, without a blueprint to guide him, he didn't know how to move the process forward. This is where I came in. I helped him to clarify his vision and create action steps towards achieving his objectives. He realized that if he truly wanted more, he had to stretch outside of himself and ask for help. He understood that change required change, and that if he really was interested in advancing his objectives to achieve more impactful results, he needed to learn a myriad of new skills. He did not know if there was a prospect of success, but he continued to persevere. He had learned early on to utilize tough times as a springboard to transform his experiences to reach new heights. Every uphill battle he experienced allowed him to assimilate more skills to be added to his ongoing achievements. His innate ability to turn problems into interesting opportunities supported him as he continued to evolve.

Nurturing and gaining resilience to bounce back from the hardships in our day is key. Innovation requires the courage to take calculated risks. Failure is often a necessary step on the path to greatness. Expect failure, remain committed to your values and beliefs, stay focused, and persevere. The most effective leaders gain insight even when they stumble. Overcoming the agony of defeat makes us more purposeful. Take strides to advance your path forward. To expand your reach, you will need to be brave, curious, and adaptable. Give yourself permission to do something new and different by stretching outside of your comfort zone.

Top Nuggets of Wisdom

1 Failure is often a necessary step on the path to greatness. Expect failure, remain committed to your values and beliefs, stay focused, and persevere.

2 People change when they are ready, willing, and able to – when it becomes their highest priority.

3 As leaders of our life, we are responsible for our own happiness; we need to be intentional about how we take care of ourselves.

CHAPTER 5

Struggling

Life is a monopolizing kaleidoscope of events. With that comes a mosaic of personal endeavors variegated in complexity. Temptations, trials, and tribulations impact all human beings no matter how much or how little fame, fortune, freedom, power, or fulfillment we appear to have. A homeless person may be thoroughly enjoying living with a sense of wonder while a multimillionaire may hate getting out of bed in the morning.

Struggles erupt when we least expect them. Intense struggles bring about unbelievably difficult days, weeks, months, and even years. These life challenges are often diverse. They can feel all-consuming. They can be devastating. The darkness surrounding these situations can be overwhelming, and it may feel as if these trials are beyond the limits of possibilities that can be overcome. It often feels as if there is no end in sight, bringing total havoc into our everyday world.

Negative thoughts activate venomous brainwork. The daunting stories we create in our minds oftentimes reflect cynicism, failure, and a deep fog of constriction. These lethal thoughts immobilize and block our passage to peace of mind.

Through hardship, starting from the moment we are born, strength and growth emerge from the depth of pain, suffering, and hard work which is needed to overcome our personal battles. The pits of relationships, financial problems, traumatic events, feeling unsafe or threatened, and the death or serious illness of a loved one, all create somber states of emotion. Encountering a range of experiences helps to provide us with practical wisdom to support us over the course of time. The challenge of human existence is our ability to consciously build awareness, while extracting the purpose and value from each struggle for the benefit of our own personal growth.

Many people feel sorry for themselves to the point of feeling victimized by their struggles. They frequently look for someone or something to blame. When we feel victimized and blame outwardly, we activate the creation of our own tales of woe, which decreases our confidence and causes us to get stuck in a vicious cycle of toxicity. These negative biases are disempowering. Alternatively, reframing the way we think about our troubles is essential. Instead of feeling that you are the victim of your circumstances, take responsibility for how you respond to your struggles. You are the only one who can change your consciousness. When you find yourself stuck in a vortex of negativity, allow yourself permission to focus on the pearls of happiness in your life versus the dolefulness of your situation. Acute physical or emotional suffering is not easy – far from it. Even though struggles can push us to our limits, do not surrender. You are not your struggles – don't let them control or limit you.

We cannot dictate all aspects of our life; however, we can have the opportunity to control how we respond even in the height of stressful times. If we are motivated and determined, we can build upon the infinite capacity of the human potential. Living with intention to overcome the full spectrum of life's obstacles requires putting aside our pride to center our attention on the promise of growth despite all of the struggles. We may not be able to change the circumstances in the moment, but we can change our thoughts about it, and our approach going forward. Positive elements create gravitational velocity, which brings a pendulum swing to strengthen affirmative results. To bring beneficial improvements into your life, pay attention to and adopt a positive thinking frame of mind. The more experience, expanded learnings, and accumulated achievements we have, the more precision we have to accommodate our struggles.

Human progress feeds on optimism. Struggles build our character. There is immeasurable good that comes from breaking through our struggles. Our aptitude, mental resilience, and agility – "inner strength", as it's often referred to – do not come from the winning moments in our lives: they are nurtured from the hardships we persevere through. Frequently the moments that we are most proud of are those where we overcame adversity and accomplished something beyond our imagination. Those noteworthy events help us to learn and appreciate that we are far more proficient than we believed we could be. The most successful among us have overcome many hurdles and countless defeats.

In my late 40s, I tested positive for the same inherited gene mutation as my father and my aunt. I quickly learned that I was the very first patient at one of Boston's world-class hospitals to have CHEK2. While this was greatly helpful to this world-famous cancer center from a research perspective, there were minimal protocols and limited proven processes for me to rely upon. One of the primary cancers associated with CHEK2 is breast cancer, so the doctors recommended that it was in my best interest to be tested every six months. During one of those regular check-ups, they discovered a cluster that had not been there six months earlier. This change in my health status inflated every aspect of my life to a level of alarming intensity. The option that my stellar medical team recommended was the most extreme, yet the one that promised the best chance for longevity.

My "radical" four-year journey included a lumpectomy, followed by a bilateral mastectomy with DIEP flap reconstruction, followed by several additional surgeries associated with reconstruction, a few skin cancers in various areas, and prophylactic risk reduction surgeries. Many long-standing, difficult-to-deal-with side effects were associated with each. I've had cancers and abnormal cell growths removed. I've had significant amounts of skin, fat, and muscle, including its blood supply, transferred to other parts of my body. I've also had a few serious wound infections, as well as temporary organ dysfunction after surgery, most of which thankfully went away as I healed.

Pain is an expected outcome of any surgery. During my surgical recoveries, I endured a tremendous amount of physical pain, often caused by my own intentional avoidance of the heavy-duty prescription-strength pain medications because they made me feel physically and psychologically ill. I often sucked up the pain, what I referred to as "white-knuckling the pain," as much as I could withstand. There was no easy solution; I experienced awful side effects when I was taking the painkillers, yet I physically suffered when I wasn't taking them. This torment was especially challenging during the most invasive and extensive surgical recoveries.

I never imagined that I would have to cope with so many surgeries, doctors' appointments, tests, and procedures, all while raising a family, growing my young businesses, and fighting through a myriad of medical obstacles and intense financial hardships. Solopreneurs and often entrepreneurs do not get sick leave, which creates its own sense of challenges, not only from a financial viewpoint but also from a business growth and development perspective. When there is a need for an extended medical leave, it creates quite a struggle, as it often causes a huge impact on the business and the entrepreneur. Even the best-laid plans made by the smartest people can get turned around unexpectedly.

Even though there were many times that I recall being desperately sick of being sick and incredibly tired of being so tired, throughout the whole ordeal, I did my best to go into each surgery with the best state of physical and emotional health. My focus was on understanding the expected outcomes, risks, and rehabilitation while also appreciating and owning my fears and areas of concern. I was mindful of making sure I was well nourished, hydrated, and well rested so that my body could use as much energy as possible to help with the healing process. Additionally, I did my best to keep up on getting groceries in the house, the bills paid on time, the laundry done in a reasonable amount of time, and the house as clean as was possible under the circumstances. Though it was extra-demanding, my project management skills combined with my forward thinking and planning abilities served my family and me well during these agonizing times.

I was persistent about putting on my sunglasses as they had rose-colored lenses – intentionally. The difference in vibrancy between rose-colored lenses and gray-tinted lenses is remarkable. I would encourage you to seek out the difference yourself. Many times, I would put on those rose-tinted sunglasses to recalibrate my mindset. In my isolated recovery space, I found it difficult to focus on anything besides my hardships. I actively repositioned my thoughts with a grateful attitude. Gratitude can help us cope and it has the power to bring us hope.

I remember many times, during the height of the most complex of my surgeries, feeling isolated, alone, lonely, stressed, anxious, and depressed, all of which are completely out of character for me. Fear of the unknown while I was in the midst of physical and emotional turmoil was wreaking havoc with my mind. I recognized the need to do something about it. I powered up my grit to re-engage with society, even with several surgical dressings of various shapes and sizes still in place. It's amazing what clothing can hide. As I re-entered my outside world, I kept focusing on maintaining a positive mindset even though I felt as if those around me had x-ray vision and could see everything I was trying to camouflage. I worked diligently to regularly show up as my best self. Since my surgeries were not back-to-back, I had to slim down my client base because I knew I wouldn't be able to support them at the level that I wanted to. I did not want my personal or professional brand to be compromised due to my ongoing medical situation. When the timing was right, each time I re-engaged in my business, I was determined to make sure I was adding value. My main focus was to make sure that I was able to provide a high-quality, focused environment to expand leadership and business performance for my clients. My strategy was to rest as much as I could before and after every client meeting. I did this faithfully.

A few months after my eleventh surgical procedure, my husband's family was going on a ski trip in Vermont. I enjoy the energy and camaraderie of skiing with family and friends as well as appreciating the breathtaking views from the summit. This ski trip was a test for me to see how my body would respond with so much scar tissue and so many surgical markers still intentionally inside my body. I've never been a great skier, but I could always navigate my way down the mountain. My mind had a certain technique for which I expected my body to respond while I was on the slopes, but my body had a whole different response. I was so thankful for my physically fit husband. He was incredibly patient and stayed the course with me even though it took almost two hours to get from the summit to the lodge. I made it through one run before I was exhausted. My body was completely out of shape. Many of the muscles I had always relied on to ski had been compromised in one way or another during the various surgeries. This was incredibly discouraging, but also illuminating at the same time. I had hoped that my skills hadn't plummeted as much as they had. My lack of strength and physical ability was disappointing, and yet it was a slap of reality for how much things had changed for me. I remember thinking to myself, "OK, it is what it is and now I have a better idea what I'm dealing with." I have had more than my share of struggles, so I am trying to be patient with myself as I gradually redevelop my muscles and my physical endurance. I am committed to being back on the slopes again with better results. I look forward to the magnificent panoramic snow-covered views from the summit.

My cancer journey consisted of an infinite number of surgical incisions. I also had needles, tubes, or wires in all areas of my body from the tips of my fingers to the bottoms of my feet to the top of my head, and everywhere in between. The most significant area impacted has been my entire front torso. The character-building physical scars are vast, but I'm learning to accept them as a badge of honor for what I have persevered through. I have survived, and I am thriving.

My objective was to do "whatever it took" to have sustainable health: to get back to myself and to feel better. I was naive to think that I would ever be back to myself. The changes that I physically and emotionally endured brought me to a higher level of understanding and appreciation for life. I'm still learning to accept my new normal. Many parts of my body are and will remain numb for the rest of my life. I remember feeling this way when I had my two emergency C-sections four years apart from each other. This most recent host of procedures permanently changed me even more both physically and emotionally. It provided a whole new meaning to the words "foreign," "strange," and "odd."

My forward planning activities prior to and while recovering from my surgeries included completely detaching from any and all news. The only thing I listened to was calming or upbeat instrumental music. I isolated myself from any negativity. I hope I do not have to be wheeled into another operating room in my lifetime, but if I do I will approach it in the same way I always have – with diligence for a better tomorrow.

My intention in sharing my story is not to seek out pity, praise, or empathy. We all have our own narrative. There are many people in our world that have far more challenging situations than I do. Situational awareness is the ability to identify, process, and comprehend what is going on around us and responding appropriately. When we expand situational awareness through storytelling, it becomes a powerful way to share insight and generate a wave of action through changes in our attitudes and behaviors. People enjoy stories because they give us permission to relate to others more effectively by forging emotional connections. I believe we would achieve different outcomes if we capitalized on storytelling more frequently as adults. It supports collaborative commerce by invoking enhanced emotional engagement that ultimately leads to greater performance.

Life is full of difficulties and misfortunes that are packaged in varying degrees of magnitude. Whether we like it or not, professional and personal hardships are part of our journey. Some of us struggle more than others and only learn when we fall hard. Nightmarish moments cause significant burden and suffering. Getting back on track after, or while still dealing with, terrifying times with a renewed sense of purpose and resolve is not easy.

There are times when things happen without warning. How we evolve after these experiences is the real indicator of our character and strength. Ironically, the optimal times to gain a deeper understanding of ourselves may come during the messiest stages of our lives. We can all be certain that there will be turbulence in our future. Usually, when we least expect it, there will be a bump in the road and trouble will emerge that will wreak havoc with our status quo. Building up our resilience so that we can face adversity is beneficial especially when we are dealing with complex problems. Concentrating on the positives will help us to enjoy the rollercoaster ride of life. Those of us who are optimistic thinkers don't keep our heads in the sand and ignore life's less than favorable situations. Instead, we approach unsavory challenges in a more absolute and productive way, without going to the extreme of being blindly optimistic. Our adaptability can be a springboard for coming up with new and creative solutions. Learning to respond with a constructive mindset to our momentous challenges expands our emotional strength, courage, character, and perseverance.

Every obstacle we successfully confront serves to strengthen our will, our confidence, and our ability to conquer barriers in the future. Many of us have a Ph.D. from the University of Hard Knocks – I know that I do. Some of these experiences we have control over and others we don't. It is important to remember that these difficult times can also help us to replenish ourselves.

We all need to make choices on how we "show up" in the face of adversity. We should live our lives in ways that resonate best with our ambitions. Our lives are happening now – they are not happening tomorrow, or next week, or next year, or even some day. Life is not meant to be passive. Waiting for someone else to take control of our lives is not progress and it does not lead to success.

When I experience difficult times, I use the image of walking up a hill. I look at the top of the hill so that I know where I am headed. My focus then goes to looking down at my feet. I start out by taking the few steps that are in front of me, and then continue to move forward, progressing steadily, and before long I am at the top of the hill. Reaching that pinnacle, I take a deep breath and look back at what I have accomplished. I smile and think to myself, "I did it!" That two-second acknowledgment and celebration helps to build confidence for what is yet to come.

We build who we are and what we become by every step we take, every sight we see, all the words that we have heard, as well as those that we have spoken throughout our lifetime. No one knows what your eyes have seen, what your heart has felt, or what you have had to walk through. Every challenge you have overcome adds content to the quality and grit of who you are today. It is important to capitalize on those experiences, both good and bad, to be able to propel your life forward. Our current feelings, personality traits, and behaviors have been shaped by our distant and recent past. Many of the challenges, perceptions, judgments, wisdom, intellect, and social skills that were formed since childhood significantly impact our lives now. Even those experiences that seemed inconsequential at the time may have a dramatic impact on our decisions today.

Our thoughts dictate what we achieve; if we have a "can do" spirit we have a better chance of persevering and accomplishing our intentions. Self-talk is the constant flow of unspoken thoughts that race through our minds. It is an important internal monologue. These thoughts can be positive or negative. Some of this mental activity comes from logic and reason, while some comes from our misconceptions and fears. If we tell ourselves that we do not have the abilities to achieve something, it sets boundaries on our accomplishments. Focus on building your life by your choices versus the hope of a windfall. Turn your thoughts from perceived scarcity to anticipated abundance. Shift your attention to appreciate what you already have versus feeling stressed about all that you do not have.

To fuel achievement, we need to concentrate on opportunities for growth. We all have different views of what we mean when we talk about effort. Regardless of our perspective, putting forth more effort, while taking calculated risks, is guaranteed to increase learning and performance. Our level of consistent effort will move the lever of progress accordingly. Increasing brain power along with toughness allows for more advanced challenges, accomplishments, and satisfaction. When we are struggling, electing to make the effort to stretch ourselves may initially feel uncomfortable and even scary, but growth requires change and change is very rarely smooth.

When the going gets tough, there is an urgent need to hyper-focus our attention. Our efforts need to be redirected from our normal schedule into the murkiness of the situation at hand. When the timing is best, remind yourself to scale back so you do not burn out.

We all have a wheel of emotions in our lives. There are times where we must force ourselves to move beyond frustration, anger, resentment, shock, and sadness if we want something better for our lives. Emotion plays a significant role in driving our human nature, especially when there are traumatic events associated with it. Memories can be abiding and powerful; they can drive behavior for a long time.

The founder of a family business was having some ongoing challenges with being too bold and not interacting respectfully with others. This "showed up" in the form of communication challenges with family members who were in the business with him. Transitioning any family business from one generation to the next comes with an intense amount of pressure, but this family's unique dynamics led to many of their altercations becoming violent. I was brought in to assess skills, influence better decisions, and support productive actions forward while also mediating the undesirable situation.

Conflict is unavoidable. Even people who are in the very best of relationships do not agree on everything. Skirmishes don't need to turn into explosive interactions. Flashpoints of conflict can erupt rapidly and can cause extra pressure and derailment from aspirations. Friction between individuals can lead to fiery, uncomfortable, and unproductive outcomes. When not managed properly, these conflicts can make or break a family and its business.

It was clear to me from the outset that there was a very real struggle taking place; it was paramount for the family members to master the essential skills that were necessary to keep their personal feelings out of all of their business decisions. This is a very complex challenge, especially in family businesses. They needed to learn, and then to agree, to put the company first during on-the-job hours if they were to achieve success both personally and professionally. Their goal was to be able to sit at the Thanksgiving dinner table together without holding grudges or resentment towards each other, while also making traction in the business. One exceptionally beneficial recommendation that I made was to create a code-word that they could all use when things intensified and became dangerously heated. This code-word had a customized meaning behind it that they all agreed to ahead of time. If someone used that word then it meant –

STOP, things are out of control, we need to take a time out to breathe and decompress. Everyone involved respected the code-word, which allowed all family members to take the time that they each needed to unwind. Once calmer minds prevailed, they were able to work through their differences of opinion. They were truly electrified to have access to this powerful tool for when a situation became high risk. They continue to have this technique in their back pocket should the need arise. It is still used, just not as frequently as it was at the beginning. More gets accomplished when we unite as opposed to fight.

Life struggles are inevitable. Expect rough seas as you voyage through your journey. Intentionality, diligence, and mental toughness will move your level of progress in the right direction. Wisdom is procured, often in unexpected ways, when we overcome considerable challenges.

Top Nuggets of Wisdom

1 Our thoughts dictate what we achieve; if we have a "can do" spirit we have a better chance of persevering and accomplishing our intentions.

2 We all need to make choices on how we "show up" in the face of adversity. We should live our lives in ways that resonate best with our ambitions.

3 Temptations, trials, and tribulations impact all human beings no matter how much or how little fame, fortune, freedom, power, or fulfillment we appear to have.

CHAPTER 6

Disruptors

Disruptors are frequently viewed as perplexing and intrusive activities, events, processes, or situations. Disruptive times can literally uproot and change how we think, learn, behave, and deal with our regular encounters. Drastic change, anticipated or not, produces various levels of impact that can range from causing some degree of disorder to causing complete turmoil. The result is that our lives are shaken up, often with the need to recast in the blink of an eye.

Disruption requires us to either pivot sideways from our routines, step backwards in our progress, or head down a less than favorable path to ultimately move forward. Disruption frequently conjures up connotations of being disgruntled due to the unsaddling of regularity. If positioned in our minds accordingly, working through disruption has the power to add value from a cumulative and compounding effect, creating beneficial learning. Coupled with grit and a positive mindset, the more experiences we are able to master by overcoming disruptors, the more seasoning we will have to support us in all aspects of our future.

The mere thought of a disruptor can bring forth excitement for some individuals, while others feel an overflowing rush of terror. Disruption often involves responding to mayhem and then overturning the situation to create something new and better. Problem-solving and change management are at the forefront of the primary tasks needed in working through disruptors. Surviving and thriving, whether they are planned, accidental, or forced disruptors, depend upon a variety of character traits in both our personal and our professional lives. Our purpose and our values, coupled with our personality and our ambitions, are deciding factors in how, or if, we are able to persevere successfully through disruptors.

As demanding as these types of events can be, most people can process through the disruptors in a productive and functional way; however, some individuals find themselves unable to cope. When we wallow in our misery and try to avoid disruptive situations, it only escalates the circumstances. Significant disruption can feel overpowering: consider a deer caught in the headlights of a car, transfixed and in harm's way. When our world is crumbling all around us, it can feel very scary and extremely isolating. On one level, it is comforting to know that we are not alone: disruptors are all around us, occurring every second of every day to multitudes of people. Over the years, several of my clients have appreciated knowing that there are many other people who are also dealing with these escalated levels of pandemonium. When we are engulfed in turbulence, it can be beneficial to ask for help. I am one of those people who finds it difficult to ask for help, but I am learning to do just that. I would encourage you to open your heart and your mind to let people in. I have found that most people are willing to help. We all have moments of intensity that can benefit from the empathy and encouragement of others. It behooves us to grant them the opportunity to spread their kindness of support.

I do not know a single person who hasn't been affected adversely by harm or injury: we have all been a victim. Healing the pain by letting go and moving forward is the emotionally healthy and healing thing to do. Knowing that the victim mentality creates a whirlwind of added challenges, try to be conscious of any tendency towards establishing a dysfunctional mindset. This is often where people seek to self-persecute in an effort to gain attention or try to avoid responsibility. Those who struggle with the "poor-me" attitude seem to convince themselves that life is well beyond their control. This pessimistic view tends to result in regular finger-pointing along with "pity parties" that are fueled by anger and fear. We need to be accountable for our own actions and responsibilities. When we continue to feel sorry for ourselves, we travel to an unproductive dark side. When we show up as a constant sufferer, whether our circumstances are real or imagined, we become high-maintenance to those who are around us. Healthy relationships can become strained and irrevocably tarnished by the twists and turns of emotional manipulators.

My daughter and I were very excited to plan a "girls' night out" together. Nurturing our family bond is a top priority for me, and I do my best to instill that in her for the benefit of our future generations. With my daughter being busy at college, and me being absorbed with growing my businesses and writing this book, we had a reduced amount of quality time together. We were thrilled to be able to secure tickets to a sold-out country music show and excited to create another happy memory together by enjoying the performances of these highly regarded musicians.

We arrived early so that we could find our seats and thereby avoid the potential of any last-minute disturbances that a late arrival would have caused. Unfortunately, the people who had tickets in the row directly in front of us arrived well after the musicians took the stage. This family of four comprised a mother, a father, and two adult daughters, both of whom appeared to be in their early to mid-30s. The older of the two girls was visibly distraught, appearing to be overwhelmed by her own tales of woe. The agitated daughter took turns emotionally erupting with each of her family members. At one point, while the mother and the other sister were enjoying themselves by giggling and dancing, the tightly wound daughter became increasingly flustered and completely discharged her state of anger on her father.

As outsiders, finding ourselves unexpectedly front and center with another family's messiness was uncomfortable, yet it was hard to ignore the disruptive outbursts. We remained empathetic and curious. I found myself splitting my attention between actively watching and listening attentively to the performance and trying to understand why this young woman was acting so out of sorts in such a public manner. Focusing on her further, I noticed that she was wearing a wig, that her skin had an unhealthy pallor, and that her slender frame bordered on emaciated. As hard as it was to do, I remained non-judgmental. There was clearly much more going on with this young woman than we would ever know. Her family tried several different approaches to de-escalate the situation, but her open display of bad behavior had reached an unmanageable state. It was at that point that her parents, though visibly fraught with embarrassment, stepped up as leaders and reined in the situation. Together, they made the difficult decision to abruptly leave the concert as a way to put a temporary lid on their older daughter's severe emotional distress.

While my daughter and I were driving home from the concert, I leveraged the opportunity to share a teachable moment. I explained to her that although we cannot control situations that happen around us, we do have the ability to curb what we allow into our lives. Therefore, it is important to be leaders of our own lives in order to have a more powerful influence over our own destiny.

Traumatic events can be devastating. These types of incidents may cause physical, emotional, and even spiritual damage. Disruptors like this can be from one single occurrence, or they can come from a number of episodes which compound to threaten an individual's safety. These alarming situations are often caused by physical agony, an attack, a violation, or loss of personal control. It could also occur when we are a witness to a serious situation that involves someone else being harmed, or being in distress, or even their untimely death. Examples of this include someone being the victim of a crime, the death of a loved one, a house fire, a car accident, a natural disaster, or even someone falling off a ladder. Our world can feel like it stops abruptly when we come upon a serious life disruption; the shock, the disbelief, the confusion, and the fear can be all-consuming.

Nerve-racking interruptions have the power to transform our lives in a positive or a negative way. There is always wisdom to be gained by the thunderclouds of hard times. On some occasions, the learning is easy to identify, while other times it is extremely difficult to uncover. Self-reflection helps us to expand our awareness. Everything that happens to us should be viewed as a life lesson: an opportunity to increase our knowledge as well as our abilities.

My daily regimen in corporate America was highly productive, but with that came a flip side that was habitually demanding and draining. This created a life that was out of balance where I yearned for more joy. My intuition told me that there was something better out there if I had the courage, motivation, and perseverance to take a giant leap of faith. I started down the uncharted path of figuring out what it would take to make my dream career a reality. My inner voice told me not only that it was too hard and too risky, but also that it was irresponsible. However, I leveraged my internal strength to continue to expand my ideas and to create a conservative business plan to move things forward. I innately knew that I had the talent to succeed, the courage to fail, the wisdom to learn, and the resilience to bounce back even stronger after any setback. This was the clarity that I needed to jump the final emotional hurdle and reach for my dream – making a favorable impact on the lives of others by supporting business leaders to accelerate success by challenging the status quo.

My clarity was short-lived. The day after I left my corporate job to become an entrepreneur, my husband fell backwards off of a ladder and landed on our brick walkway. I heard a loud thud, ran out the front door, and saw him lying motionless with blood coming out of the back of his head. The tailspin of crushing stress was insurmountable. My initial thought was that he was dead. I screamed to our two teenage kids to call 911. My thoughts kept going to, "What if he doesn't survive?" and then these ramblings bled straight into, "How am I going to financially support our kids?" Even though I knew that it was time for me to leave my job, I had just given away my security. I was internally beating myself up for taking the risk for a better future for all of us. My gremlins were asking me, "Why didn't you just find another corporate job instead of starting a new business with no security? What are you going to do?" Gloomy hypothetical scenarios were rapidly going through my mind. I reminded myself that this defeatist thought process was not adding value, but instead was creating even more stress and greater emotional despair. I needed to refocus and step up as the shepherd of our family. Focusing on the positive was paramount because our kids were taking their cues from me. As difficult as it was, I leaned into the key role that I needed to show up for, which was to not only support my kids, but to also support my husband in the best way possible even though I was extremely fearful of the unknown. After what seemed like an eternity, the medical team informed us that my husband was alive. We learned that he had broken his back and that he had several staples in his head. He was in a form-fitted rigid back brace for almost three months. It was a long and intense road back to recovery.

I was fully committed to his rehabilitation and well-being. I had planned appropriately from a financial perspective to ramp up my business. It had never been a forethought that the timing to build my business would be altered and financially impacted by an unexpected serious accident. Once my husband could self-manage and his pain had reduced, I knew the time was right to start moving the business forward. There was so much to learn, so many decisions to make, and so many bumps along the way. It was a difficult road, and at times it was painstakingly hard to stay the course. Even though I had planned for a conservative timeline, everything took significantly longer to accomplish. The unfamiliar things that popped up created the need for ongoing interventions, all of which required added time and a further commitment to overcome.

Disruptive events rarely happen at convenient moments. Life can be extreme, abrupt, and unpredictable, and we all react differently to every situation. Not many people or organizations have the support system and/or financial resources to hit the life equivalent of a pause button until these issues are resolved. Some extreme circumstances define and paralyze us, while others find a way to awaken our energy to strive for a better quality of life. We cannot always control what happens to us; however, we can call the shots on how we bounce back. By making small positive tweaks to our inner voice, we can have a major impact on how we respond during adversity. I would like to underscore the importance of concentration and perseverance when presented with our own murky challenges.

Life can be tangled and chaotic. Turbulent periods of time can seem mammoth in size and often wreak havoc on us. During these difficult times, life can grip us incredibly hard and we can feel very single-handed, and yet it is during these most difficult times that we are provided with invaluable wisdom. Some people don't like to wear their heart on their sleeve, and yet they may be the very people who are struggling the most. I happen to be one of those people who has had uphill battles for most of my life.

During my cancer recovery, I was invited to attend a dinner meeting comprising high-powered entrepreneurs. Even though I hadn't healed from my most recent surgery, I thought it would be a good opportunity to promote my business. Since birth, I have always had severe food allergies. They can be life threatening if I even touch a peanut or any type of tree nut. From a planning perspective, it was confirmed multiple times that all of the food to be served at the dinner was free of my allergens. Even with various safety nets in place, I was exposed to minor amounts of almonds and almond oil in the salad. I went into anaphylactic shock. Though this is a life-threatening situation for anyone, in my case emergency resuscitation would damage the most recent reconstructive surgery and inhibit the healing process. Saving my life became the priority. Fortunately, I remained conscious and they stabilized me without resuscitation.

Although this incident was one of the most intense experiences I have ever encountered, I never considered myself a victim, nor did I feel sorry for myself. I didn't want this occurrence to define who I was or to limit my path forward. I would encourage you to choose as I did, should you ever find yourself in an extreme circumstance. I gave myself an inspirational jolt, which forced me to put my best self forward, and bravely lean into the experience I was forced to endure. My thoughts were better spent focusing on next steps and how to move through this grisly life experience in the best way possible. Thankfully life goes on even after a severely frightening, near-death illness.

One thing that I have finally come to terms with is that I cannot control everything in my life. For years, I tried to do just that. The need to control created agitation, unnecessary pressure, and many sleepless nights. In a broader context, learning what we can control and what is out of our control is paramount to being able to focus on those things that we can fine-tune to best navigate our expedition. At times, we are completely blindsided by unexpected bumps in the road. Sometimes, we can reduce the surprise by being more proactive, more present, and more aware. We can choose to view problems as having the good fortune to teach ourselves and others about imagining possibilities. We can seek out solutions while suspending judgment. Experiences allow us the consistent latitude to learn and shine, while also allowing for a powerful domino effect of accomplishment.

Disruptors can be positive in nature. They can be creative and healthy for individuals as well as for organizations. Those people who are positive disruptors seek out opportunities for improvement. These visionary and innovative thinkers look to raise the bar of accomplishment even higher. Transformative change is about unleashing our drive and our abilities to achieve a higher level of satisfaction with solutions that are focused on making our best even better.

A positive disruptor can also be someone who challenges crusty habits and works to find beneficial alternatives. Those with an innovative mindset are relentless in making forward moves. They impact the shift of fundamental behaviors and expectations. A positive disruption displaces a culture, a market, an industry, or a technology by producing something new that is worthwhile and more efficient.

There will always be people who resist change. In many cases, they put up a fight because they are afraid of failure: fear of the unknown is paralyzing to them. To successfully navigate proactive disruption, human dynamics needs to be seriously taken into consideration at every step in the process. Personal and professional optimization happens when there is a high level of trust. Visionary leaders create the necessary conditions for innovation to flourish.

Changemakers are those among us who are tenacious about consciously activating solutions to expand the greater good. They are innovators who have a deep-rooted sense of purpose to tackle and resolve major challenges. Changemakers are comfortable stepping outside of their comfort zone. They thrive on meaningful action for purpose – on purpose.

To create a raw burst of navigational change, intentionally seek out and listen to people who provoke and challenge your thoughts with a primary objective of maximizing untapped opportunities and potential. When we design and drive for scale, it allows us to go beyond the ambitions of incremental impact. There are an infinite amount of possibilities accessible to us when we view life through a visionary's mentality. Create seismic change by harnessing the power of disruptors. Shift wisely to unlock trapped value into advantageous returns.

Top Nuggets of Wisdom

1 Our purpose and values coupled with our personality and ambitions are deciding factors in how or if we persevere successfully through disruptors.

2 If positioned in our minds accordingly, working through disruption has the power to add value from a cumulative and compounding effect, creating beneficial learning.

3 Changemakers are those among us that are tenacious about consciously activating solutions to expand the greater good.

CHAPTER 7

Kryptonite

I believe that most people are inherently good; I believe in humankind. I also believe that tumultuous times usually erupt due to the radioactive elements within us that we all know as: "Kryptonite."

Our mind guides our course such that our life is a direct reflection of our mental framework. Our brain is so powerful; it is at the center of who we are. It is where our perceptions, thinking, awareness, decision-making, and memory come from. More specifically, it is the home for our thoughts, feelings, attitudes, assumptions, and creative resourcefulness. All of which help us to form our viewpoints, approaches, and convictions. Our deficiencies in these areas show up as our Achilles heels and become our personal and professional kryptonite, hindering our energy for achievement.

Kryptonite seizes us in a variety of ways. What we do and do not do has a positive or negative consequence to us as well as to those who we are connected to. It is impossible to compare our own problems or our own lives with those of others, even though we try to do it all the time. Life should never be a competition to see "who has it worse." Problems quake different people in different ways. What may be a relatively inconsequential event for one person could be a life-changing disaster for someone else. Everyone is deserving of consideration for their hardships. As leaders of our own lives, we are each responsible for our own actions, regardless of the problems we have come up against in the past or ones we are currently grappling with.

I've found that people often assume that they have a realistic sense of self; however, there are many among us who do not realize that they are deficient in an objective view of self-awareness and self-direction. The growing number of disengaged in our population do not appear to think about or even care if they are effective in their everyday life. Having an accurate calibration of our natural self is the attribute that is needed for self-analysis of our true identity. To optimize our fortitude through achievement, we need to slow down to speed up. When we give ourselves permission to go "offline" from our everyday activities, we can better activate our untapped brain energy.

To overcome the "hit the snooze" mentality requires upgrading our body's ability to rest and create energy: improving brain functionality. The specifics of this type of strategy will be completely different for each of us, but often include an improved level of health specifically in the areas of rest, relaxation, eating, and exercise. The mental aspect of quarterbacking our own lives is tough to do. When we gain insight and make simple changes, we can increase our focused mental acuity and thus create the opportunity to achieve more and better.

Our ultimate weaknesses are disempowering and all-consuming, and when left unchecked they can contribute to many life and health complications. They also have detrimental behavior and performance effects. Our weaknesses are displayed most often in negative self-talk, narcissistic attitudes, obsessive behaviors, deeply rooted bad habits, debilitating thought patterns, and toxic relationships. These attitudes and actions often show up as anxiety, fear, stress, procrastination, distractibility, self-sabotage, and/or judgmentalism.

Most of us have physical and/or emotional battle scars caused by our everyday lives. It is important to remember that we are more than our scars. They do not define us; they do, however, contribute to who we are. Our vulnerabilities are weaknesses that we can improve upon if we choose to. No matter how deep our difficulties appear, we need to be able to understand our own strengths and weaknesses to cultivate peace of mind. It is easy for us to get trapped within our own self-limiting loop. You have the innate power to detach yourself from swimming in a sea of despair. Instead, take back control by reducing the grip your debilitating tendencies have over you. Real transformation can only occur when we get to the core of what is holding us back. To improve our immunity, we need to deeply immerse ourselves into a better comprehension of when and why we do the things that we do.

Emotional wounds associated with our individual kryptonite(s) can run deep, with some planted deeper than others. These wounds can cause good people to get stuck in destructive patterns of behavior or ruinous situations. The latitude and longitude of these circumstances can impact our entire sense of self. When we are brutally honest with ourselves, we can identify our critical flaws. Once identified, we can learn to increase our power over our kryptonite so that we can better manage, rather than threaten, our well-being.

To boost resilience, I would encourage you to cast a more positive light on your strengths instead of focusing on your faults or imperfections. If we choose to consistently center our spotlight on the good in us, while still being attentive to our shortcomings, our self-image will gradually be improved. It takes positive thinking, preparation, and repetitional efforts to gain or regain our sense of worth and progress. To become more expansive, look for opportunities to appreciate and affirm your most valuable attributes. Doing this will help to strengthen your sense of self-worth and support you as you wrestle with your existing and new circumstances.

We will never know what our true upper limits are unless we get off the merry-go-round of wasted opportunities. Being able to recognize our kryptonite symptoms can give us an upturn on managing them. This chapter will highlight the primary areas of kryptonite that I witness most often when working with others.

Top Nuggets of Wisdom

1 Our deficiencies show up as our Achilles heels and become our personal and professional kryptonite: radioactive and binding our energy for achievement.

2 Our ultimate weaknesses are disempowering and all-consuming. Left unchecked, they can contribute to many life and health complications.

3 Most of us have physical and/or emotional battle scars arising from our everyday lives. We are more than our scars. They do not define us; they do, however, contribute to who we are.

PART 1

Procrastination And Distractibility

Like all forms of kryptonite, chronic procrastination and distractibility negatively impact our overall quality of life. Easily being diverted away from, or the intentional delay of, completing tasks or activities is widespread. The lack of maintaining attention on the necessary action items in our everyday world causes a pile-up of delays. The intensity of juggling deferred tasks often leads to stress, anxiety, physical and mental exhaustion, lowered self-esteem, damaged relationships, and academic/career setbacks. Due to a deep-rooted fear of failure, some people get emotionally debilitated, and thereby live in continuums. Apprehension, embarrassment, guilt, and regret get us into a rut and we can lose our way. When this happens, learning, achieving, and self-efficiency are usually critically impacted.

When our life feels as if it is on hold, we are the only ones who can actually reboot and nudge ourselves forward. For some people this holding pattern can be days, months, or even years of being stuck in a self-induced pause mode. The path ahead may appear daunting, but when we approach it calmly and cautiously, doing small amounts at a time, we will be better able to gain the confidence and initiative to continue. If we can overcome our resistance to stand up in the face of what we are afraid of doing, we can transition from one stage to another in a healthy way. As we gain momentum in accomplishing our goals, we will begin to spiral ourselves in an upward direction.

The named partner of a New York-based law firm asked me to work with his firm to enhance its culture. Through one-to-one conversations, as well as in small group discussions with the dozen partners, it became apparent that what was really needed was an intervention at the top leadership level. The firm lacked cohesiveness in all aspects, from the lack of a company mission and vision, to the lack of a strategic plan that everyone could agree upon. There were fundamental differences across the board. We discussed the overarching challenges that the firm faced and reviewed the requisite phases and timeline to move it forward. Sadly, the firm's partners were not willing to devote the time, the money, or the effort to make the vital changes that would enhance the firm as well as its employees' quality of work life.

Procrastinators are unwilling or unable to acknowledge that not deciding is still a decision: it is a decision not to change. Most of the time they don't change because the pain of change is more uncomfortable than keeping things the way they are – even if the environment is toxic and it ravages the bottom line. This firm's procrastination spawned lost opportunities in employee engagement, retention, and recruitment, in addition to striking a blow to the overall profits and revenue.

I have worked with procrastinators who unabashedly deflect the ownership of the delay, and then either trivialize the activity or blame something or someone else. They may even convince themselves that the demands placed upon them are fundamentally unfair, and resolve to rebel against them. We can suffer just as much from the things that we don't do as from those that we do. On the plus side, I have witnessed businesses overcome procrastination challenges, but the efforts must be enduring. The core of procrastination is really about our aptitude for self-control and our ability to wrap our mindset around priorities. The motivation to modify must come from within us. Our thoughts and actions need to adjust if we want a different outcome.

I have witnessed people procrastinate due to fear, lack of interest, feeling overwhelmed, and not knowing when, where, or how to get started. It is very human to stall some of our decisions and actions about one thing or another, but when we put off doing what is essential, it can become a precarious situation.

With all of the advancements in technology, it is now much easier to find distractions that can offer instant gratification. For most of us, technology is a positive force that can offer us an edge, but for procrastinators it can be a huge stumbling block. Procrastinators have an internal resistance that overpowers and derails them; they cannot find the balance. Procrastinators lose track of time, fall behind, and ultimately miss out on opportunities because they didn't act in a timely manner.

If you are unable to get a handle on when and how you become preoccupied so that you do the opposite of your goals, you may be a procrastinator. If so, look to catch yourself at the very beginning of going down the "shiny object" path and redirect your efforts towards your goal. Don't give in to the avoidance behavior. For procrastinators, distractions usually hold more weight at that very moment they choose that path versus the action that they should be focusing on.

New habits take time to integrate because you are reprogramming your thoughts and patterns. This kind of behavioral change isn't easy, but it is necessary if you want a better tomorrow. Your actions must match your desire for a changeover. Your success, or lack thereof, is owned by you alone.

Often people make excuses to justify why they failed to center their attention on the most important tasks. Some people tell themselves that they are more effective when they wait until the last minute to accomplish something. How people respond to external forces varies from one person to another. Some people choose to do nothing, some become proactive, while others tend to be more reactive. It is helpful to identify and utilize coping mechanisms that work best for you to process through the difficulties of life. Depending upon what the external factors are, you may experience a call to action, or you may feel a lack of engagement. You can choose your reaction, and it will be revealed and expressed in your words, and more importantly, in your actions.

It is paramount that we keep in mind the impact of our decisions on those we hold close both personally and professionally. Have you ever waited until the very last minute to make a decision about something crucial? Postponing a decision until the very last minute unleashes a profound negative effect on others. Being in denial as a leader jars morale and employee engagement. Be mindful of the toll your lack of decision-making is establishing. Intentional or not, it pressures others to put forth unreasonable supplementary efforts. Chronic procrastination is a growing and serious problem that is ruining lives, businesses, and careers. Moving forward is a choice. It is amazing how powerful and quick behavioral shifts can happen when we are intentional about our thoughts and actions. Find the spark from within to ignite even the smallest of actions. Stretch yourself, even if you think you can't – try it. It can feel unpleasant when you are outside of your comfort zone, but consistent small wins add up and eventually render big returns.

Top Nuggets of Wisdom

1 Apprehension, embarrassment, guilt, and regret get us in a rut and we can lose our way. Learning, achieving, and self-efficiency are usually critically impacted.

2 The intensity of juggling deferred tasks often leads to stress, anxiety, physical and mental exhaustion, lowered self-esteem, damaged relationships, and academic/career setbacks.

3 Own your mistakes, make amends, and move on with the goal of beginning anew.

PART 2

Self-Sabotage

O ur mind has the ability to riddle us habitually with anxiety and fear based upon the negative thoughts and stories we tell ourselves; it can often deceive and paralyze us. Our patterns and our perceptions have been developed from our past experiences. Some of our patterns and perceptions serve us well, while others are blocking our progress towards things that we want or need. These patterns and perceptions dictate our relationship with everything in our world. If we think we are helpless and victims of our circumstances, then we are. If we think that we will not succeed, then we won't. Fear and toxic internal talk deplete our advancement and our happiness. We become what we believe. These behaviors destroy our vitality, leaving us exhausted and without connection to the powerful energy we require to shape our best self. At times, our inner voice turns against us by undermining our desires, casting doubts on our abilities, and even convincing us to be suspicious and paranoid.

As a favor to a friend, I was asked to work with an adult family member who had a deep-rooted habit of negative self-talk. He had an intense fear of failure which had created many roadblocks. This prevention of progress had hijacked his life. Over the years, it had caused him to lose his sense of self-worth, which had significantly reduced his self-esteem. Based upon his past, the story he had continued to tell himself was that he would fail at whatever job he had – so why even bother trying? During our work together, he gained a better appreciation for the certainty that the experiences from his past did not automatically own or define his future. His yesterdays could not be modified, yet his fate did not deserve to be chastised. Creating a more supportive story to carry him forward was a strange and uncomfortable concept for him. He was lukewarm in his commitment to accelerate his success because of his lack of confidence in his abilities. As a result, we agreed that he would advance gradually through mini-steps of progress. As he started to see small daily wins, he started to gain his confidence back. We celebrated these influential moments along the way. This praise helped him to rise above the intimidation and the intensity of change that he was so fearful of. He still struggles with the tendency to self-sabotage, but he now has the self-assurance and a tried and true system in place to self-manage his actions with more favorable results.

Syncing up our wants and our needs with our internal feelings and stories allows us to harness the energy that is required to empower our choices and to overcome unexpected obstacles. Rewiring our thoughts is an open-ended process. It is helpful to reinforce the good, while repairing and learning from the bad. Positive thoughts reap positive outcomes and vice versa. I would encourage you to not let your negative fearfulness self-define your path ahead. It is your choice if you allow toxic thoughts to own you, or if you choose instead to break through those mind games with positive thoughts and positive actions. Transition your mindset to focus more on what is within your control, and capitalize on that rather than letting the "what-ifs" hold you back. Only you have the absolute power over yourself.

Most of us have not put much thought into what we want our destiny to be; better yet, what we do not want it to be. Getting familiar with our own patterns of self-destruction can help us to avoid self-sabotage.

Repetitive and compulsive behaviors can be normal. When they become excessive to the point of being all-consuming and disruptive to our daily lives, that is when it transitions into a problematic fascination. No one sets out to have an extreme compulsion. Oftentimes, it is a substance or an activity that was viewed as a way to relax or increase enjoyment. Addiction is a complex fixation. It is a compulsive act of obsession that cannot be controlled or stopped. The rewarding effects provide an overpowering and irresistible desire to habitually continue the behavior in spite of detrimental consequences. It impairs our control over our relationships and our everyday activities. Often, the pleasurable effects of the addiction dominate the world of addicts and blind them to understanding that their behavior is causing various levels of harmful consequences both for them and for those around them. Addicts often justify their cravings as rewards for, or as a relief from, their perceived challenges.

Obsessions can be visible through excessive internet/smartphone overuse, gaming, pornography, sexual addiction, pyromania, stealing, cheating, gambling, substance abuse, exercising, eating, and hoarding. Compulsive desires may include risky, ritualistic, or inappropriate social activities. The physical and psychological extreme cravings for these behaviors or substances have a strong hold on the addict's body and mind. Passion is a wonderful thing, but it should be tempered with a healthy balance. Sometimes the line between passion and addiction can become fuzzy. When someone gets overly obsessed with their desires, it can turn into an addiction and often causes much self-destruction.

A devoted volunteer and entrepreneur became a client of mine. He owned two businesses, both of which were floundering, and yet he maintained that he didn't know why. Over the first few months of working with him, I noticed a pattern of inconsistencies in his behavior which I called him out on. He divulged that he had a drug addiction. He shared with me that our work together had given him a newfound sense of his own worth and that he no longer wanted to continue to live the life of an addict. I provided him with professional resources that I was aware of and he started on his path to recovery. Once he had gained a better handle on his dependency issue, we started working together again. He felt that he had a better appreciation for how his addiction was causing him to go backwards versus making traction towards what he really wanted in his life.

Our work together continued to progress notably well until an event took place that put him in a tailspin: he discovered that the longest-tenured member of his leadership team had been stealing from him for years. He was beyond shock and disbelief and admitted to being tempted to start back up on his drug of choice. I told him that I couldn't stop him from becoming a junkie again, but I requested that, before he returned to his old lifestyle, he needed to think about how he had uncovered this ongoing stealing. He said that he had been doing a deep dive into his financials, and that was when he unearthed the trail of missing money. I asked him when was the last time that he had done a financial audit. He admitted sheepishly that he never had. I asked him why he thought he had both the capacity and the desire to do this investigation now. He confessed that it was the first time that his mind had been clear enough to take on such an intense project. He knew that he had the aptitude because he was clean. I shared with him that if he had still been doing drugs, he would never have discovered that his trusted long-term employee had been stealing from him. Being clean, he possessed the range to see and digest what was going on in his businesses.

Learning of this deceit almost caused him to relapse, but he faced his liabilities and did not backslide. He allowed me to guide him on how best to move forward. He implemented the strategy perfectly, and in so doing he stepped up as the leader that we both knew he could be. The more he continued to stay focused on what he genuinely wanted, the more he knew that plunging back into drugs held no answers for him. He continues to muster additional strength to press on towards achieving his life goals.

When we are addicted to a particular activity, person, thing, or substance despite harmful consequences, it limits our life and negatively impacts those who are within our sphere. These dependencies can often be symptomatic of other underlying problems, like stress, anxiety, depression, low self-esteem, awkwardness in social situations, or loneliness. Oftentimes the addiction exacerbates these symptoms. Many people are struggling with some type of addiction in today's over-demanding and stressful society. Self-soothing is a temporary fix to attain a different state of consciousness.

When our habits become overindulging or we make ongoing unhealthy choices, it wreaks havoc in our lives. Negative circumstances can cause us to fall short of expectations. Finding a healthier way to cope with underlying problems will assist in overcoming addiction. Healing from addiction is extremely challenging. It is possible to change the direction of our life. The first steps often come with the greatest difficulty. Awareness and admitting that some behaviors have become unmanageable is an important beginning. There is a silver lining in every dark cloud. Reflect on the past but keep your focus on the future.

To better control our destiny, we need to start acting against our inner critic and break away from the defenses that no longer aid us. Once we familiarize ourselves with our defenses, we are better able to purge our self-restricting habits and counterproductive behaviors to live a more significant life.

Traditionally, low self-esteem and lack of confidence are at the heart of our self-defeating behaviors, leaving us feeling unworthy of a full life. We fall prey to our negative thinking and negative behaviors which stop us from improving. Extracting our inner strength and commitment to be solutions-driven when we are trying to overcome the "enemy from within" will reduce our self-vandalism. By shifting our words and thoughts from "I can't do this" to "I can do this," we are more likely to avoid the distractions that are self-defeating.

People self-sabotage without even realizing it. It is helpful to learn to identify and acknowledge when potholes turn into black holes to the point of causing roadblocks. To permanently remove personal sabotaging patterns from our life, we must make an effort every day to stay conscious and aware of our thoughts, our behaviors, and our actions. Reducing and even eliminating restrictive thoughts from our mind will take time. Some people are only able to do this gradually, because these long-standing behaviors have such a strong grip. Over time, you will be able to think bigger and bolder, enabling you to expand your understanding and your perspective.

I would encourage you to go off the beaten path and let your mind wander to foster your creative energy. Think about giving birth to exciting new ideas of what you can do to confront the challenges in your life to achieve more favorable outcomes. Inspiring rejuvenation in our self-direction is essential to enhance our thoughts, actions, and achievements. Life has its snags, especially when it comes to making very difficult decisions and then implementing corresponding changes. Practice being ready for the inevitable forks in the road: they represent some of life's biggest moments. Appreciating what your direction is helps you to gauge the range of possibilities that are available to you. Think about your decision-making process. It is key to having a clear understanding of your goal. Venture to be more deliberate by organizing relevant information and outlining alternatives.

Understanding the internalized story that we have created about ourselves is helpful. Some norms are deeply ingrained in us from childhood. Gaining clarity on what choices we have already made in our life based upon that inner narrative will spearhead how we each move forward. Outside influences usually play a role in our interpretation of any situation. Assess whether those views are serving you well or are hurting you and/or those around you. From time to time, it is advantageous to revisit your preconceived notions so that you can either continue to validate them or decide to challenge them. These perspectives may have served you well at one point in your life, but fresh outlooks enable us to develop and mature. Weigh your options, consider the consequences, and make the best decision based upon your ultimate objective.

Many of the moments that define each one of us have already happened. When you get derailed in a self-sabotaging way, regain your focus on the flow and pattern of your thoughts. Our minds can re-establish and better radiate a consistent vibration of positive thinking, intentions, and actions. Architect your success by raising the rest of your life to meet you where you want to be.

Top Nuggets of Wisdom

1 Our mind has the ability to riddle us habitually with anxiety and fear based on the negative thoughts and stories we tell ourselves; it can often deceive and paralyze us.

2 Syncing up our wants and our needs with our internal feelings and stories allows us to harness the energy that is required to empower our choices and to overcome unexpected obstacles.

3 Getting familiar with our own patterns of self-destruction can help us to avoid self-sabotage.

PART 3

Judgment

Some people have venom running through their veins that is often motivated, in whole or in part, by prejudice. A judgmental person is someone who gains a feeling of superiority over another person through antagonistic methods. They enjoy making snap harsh assessments out of a sense of spite. We don't really know why people make the decisions or do the things that they do. More often than not, we do not base our opinions on distinct evidence or factual knowledge – we just make the "knee-jerk" decision and believe it as if it was based on fact. The challenge with making these types of assumptions is that more times than not we are wrong. These emotional pollutants blur our own protocols, causing a ripple of poisonous effects on society.

Frequently, judgmental people are irrational and arbitrary in their point of view because they base it on their own idiosyncratic values and beliefs. Their closed-off, preconceived notions are shallow, pessimistic, and with an unempathetic, destructive purpose. Their excessively critical tendencies disparage others, even though they may be smart, productive, and accomplished people. They willfully believe that their reality is the only viewpoint that is valid. When humans perceive a person, a situation, or an environment to be the opposite of their own views, they tend to be overly critical. Their dark intentions, fueled by their insecurities, can conjure up a way to gain a seat at the table.

Having an opinion is not the same as being judgmental. We make judgments throughout the course of our days. We can and should judge from a non-harmful position: one based on pure motives. Strive to judge with integrity, as judgmentalism weakens our society. Intentionally or not, when we violate moral principles, we are acting like degenerates who live an immoral lifestyle. No two people have the same experiences, priorities, views, and interpretations. We each have different reactions to things; there will always be human differences. When we live in the unyielding space of right or wrong, good or bad, we miss out on the meaningful areas that are in between.

Going forward, when you have an opinion, try monitoring your thoughts from a place of moral consciousness. Sound judgment is a formed, common-sense opinion of how we perceive something based upon thoughtful awareness, experience, understanding, and reasoning. As we judge, it is helpful to understand and to take into consideration that we are all at various stages of personal, social, and emotional development. When we are open to evaluating all of the evidence that is in front of us in an effort to support a decision that is made by reasoning, our judgments have more quality, further sensibility, and greater compassion.

I was twelve years old, attending a small private school, and thrilled to finally be able to be in our school's chorus. Our teacher was passionate about music and had us spending a good deal of time practicing songs in preparation for a holiday event. My position was in the top row towards the right side of the room. As we sang, her face contorted, and she seemed unusually upset by something. She stopped us from singing as a group and asked, instead, for only the right side of the room to sing. Next, she narrowed things down even further and asked for just the top-right side of the room to sing. She complained that someone was not vocally reproducing the pitch properly and that she was determined to identify who it was. She called me out to sing the verse alone while everyone scowled at me. It was horrifying! It was me! I wished that there was such a thing as an invisibility cloak; I remember feeling mortified and wishing that I could just disappear. At twelve years old, I truly believed that embarrassment was something that I could die from. Even more than four decades later, the judgment from that singular moment shaped my anxiety and fear towards performance-related events. I am not alone in having trepidation about being in front of an audience. I have been fortunate that I have been able to gain control over this angst with much practice and support.

Our world is deeply deprived of generous interactions. I believe it is because judgmentalism and criticism are so rampant. No one should wield the power to degrade or devalue someone else. A judgmental mind is an outgrowth of a mean-spirited negative mind. A lot of people are judgmental without even realizing it. Many people gravitate towards what is wrong with a person, or their views, or a situation, versus what is right. Many of us pass a verdict quickly based upon knowing very little about the actual person and his or her circumstances. Every one of us has blind spots that can make us insensitive to our own tendencies towards those who are different. Subconsciously or consciously we identify people who are different from us. We naturally gravitate towards those who are like us, or to those who we have something in common with. We notice visible differences such as gender, ethnicity, age, and disability, as well as differences such as religion, education, accent, clothing style, and sexual orientation. Our awareness also identifies disparities such as beliefs, manners, attitudes, and energy levels. We all make assumptions, but when these assumptions turn into negatively judging others, this is hurtful, debilitating, and destructive. Assumptions blind us to our own weaknesses and hinder our progress. When judgment moves in, relationships deteriorate, especially when we consistently engage in a way that is overly critical and opinionated. Ironically, we make excuses for our own behavior, but when someone else does a similar thing, we can be merciless. We have the freedom to choose our attitude in relation to a situation or a person. Many people find it hard to remain neutral when there is a point of view that we find difficult to understand, or that we may even find offensive. This may require us to identify and unlearn toxic attitudes that hold us back. If we can be inquisitive about the person's experiences, and remain open to learn more about their viewpoint, there is the real possibility of a perception that will transform us.

Mistakes, misunderstandings, and spontaneous bad choices are common. No one wants to be guilty of making poor decisions or exhibiting errors in judgment, nor do we want to be misunderstood; however, these things all happen on a regular basis. We are fully capable of impacting others in a negative way with varying degrees of frequency and severity. It is when we can reflect and recognize where we have opportunities to grow that we can enlarge our consciousness and increase our effectiveness.

People have a natural tendency to break off into groups with similar interests, standards, or objectives. When we are not part of the "in crowd," there is a tendency for less than favorable behavior to emerge. Sometimes the actions are aggressive, and sometimes they are covert and subtle. These destructive behaviors often cast judgment, as the members of the group believe that their opinion is the only point of view. A tug-of-war begins, and rivalry becomes acceptable behavior. Opinions fly easily – I call it "slinging mud." Everyone has an opinion, even those who don't have the facts. People pass judgment on what others say or do without any baseline or context. Some people seek their entertainment by trying to make others feel small. I have learned that those who excessively judge others usually have low self-esteem and lack empathy. They generally have a difficult time overcoming rejection, tend to hold grudges, and harbor resentment.

During my medical battle, I was informed of the need for an unexpected additional surgery. A collection of people asked, "Is this surgery necessary? Do you have to have it?" The irony of these questions was that they came from people who knew me well. Were they of the opinion that I would just plunge into another surgery without having done a great deal of research? I found myself biting my tongue when what I really wanted to say was, "No, I just like to go under the knife for fun!" It is cruel for anyone to pass a judgment on what is and what isn't necessary in someone else's life. The hard lesson that I learned as I approached that extra surgery was to not give other people the power to disrupt my thoughts, my feelings, my actions, or my destiny. No one knows what is best for you except you.

Due to the judgmental landscape of our society, I refrained from telling most of my business contacts about what I was battling. I knew that possessing any kind of a weak link in the business world wouldn't bode well. My future business intentions required that I be able to perform at the highest level to accelerate success for clients. I needed to be taken seriously and have all "judgments" be positive in nature and based solely on my personal and professional skills and abilities. The intensity of my medical journey lasted for over four years and comprised ten complicated surgeries and ten tortuous recoveries. It was one of the loneliest and most difficult periods in my life. It was only when I had finally obtained a clean bill of health that I felt comfortable sharing what I had been through. My goal had been to protect my personal brand at all costs. I had accomplished that, but it came at a price; I did what I did because I was motivated entirely by the fear of being judged.

We have all been judged and we have all judged others. No one likes being judged. When we misjudge and misconstrue, and then share these distorted opinions with others, we not only become an offender, but we become someone who lacks moral character. Individuals who see themselves as morally superior are known to spotlight faults in everyone but themselves. Broadcasting an attitude of superiority is a shortcoming that does not serve anyone well. Having a negative attitude is sticky and hard to break away from, but our resources will always be better spent if we aspire to improve ourselves rather than assessing others in a reckless fashion. Instead of slinging mud, try gifting appreciation and praise.

Top Nuggets of Wisdom

1 Frequently, judgmental people are irrational and arbitrary in their point of view based on their own idiosyncratic values and beliefs. Their closed-off, preconceived notions are shallow, pessimistic, and with an unempathetic destructive purpose.

2 Having an opinion is not the same as being judgmental. No two people have the same experiences, priorities, views, and interpretations. Therefore, we each have different reactions to things; there will always be human differences. We can judge from a non-harmful position.

3 It is helpful to understand that we are all at various stages of personal, social, and emotional development.

PART 4

Fear

Fear is a vital survival tool in our own personal operating system. It goes into high alert when our brain perceives risk or danger. Fear is an essential component for evolution. For many of us, when we are in a state of fear, our brain supports us by coming up with thought-provoking and clever ways to carry on and prosper. For others, fear shocks our reasoning and accountability in detrimental ways. Fear can leave us susceptible to intense emotions and impulsive reactions such that we find ourselves in a place of incapacitation. Fright can cause us to feel powerless and stifle our progress. Fear factors can be real or imagined. When there is genuine or perceived danger, pain, or threat, we have a tendency to display behaviors of fleeing, hiding, or freezing up. These behaviors can wreak havoc and fill our mind with stories of doubt and anxiety. Remaining silent or ignoring problems can snowball into epic proportion. When this occurs, it creates a physical decay and degradation of motivation. Fear reduces our inspiration to achieve, preventing us from moving up the ladder of prosperity.

An executive that I had been working with for a while seemed unusually quiet and distracted during one of our sessions. He opened up to me about a situation that had been unraveling at home. He and his wife were at odds over how to deal with their son's struggles with his first year of college. Their son had been an award-winning athlete since he was very young, and had great passion for many sports. His goal was to attend a college where he could continue to play football. As a result, he was thrilled to get into his chosen college because it was known to have a great football coaching staff and a trend of successful team outcomes. He was ecstatic to be able to continue to evolve his skills with this coach and his new teammates.

This high-potential college freshman found himself in an unfortunate intense situation for which he had no experience. His chosen university required all incoming freshmen to declare their major prior to being accepted into the school. Being able to satisfy this requirement is a lot to expect of any young person with limited life experience. He had always been fascinated with engineering, so he decided his academic focus would be in that space. Shortly into his first term, he discovered, but was afraid to admit, that he had chosen the wrong area to major in. This realization, combined with his rigorous athletic schedule, was significantly more than he could cope with. This led to serious and debilitating changes in his self-care. He endured an excessive amount of rapid weight loss, he constantly overslept, he missed his classes, and he eventually fell behind in his school work. Before his first term was over, he had fallen so far behind that he had to drop out of school and move back home. Once back home, he isolated himself from everything and everyone. Several months after his parents had numerous heart-to-heart conversations with him about his need to do more than be secluded in his bedroom, he realized that his academics were the main reason that he was going to college. With a heavy but more mature heart, he gave up football and decided to make his sole focus attaining a college education. He made a few more attempts at various local colleges, but this resulted in little to no success. He was exhausted by his own distress and became even more emotionally paralyzed with fear – fear of failure.

My client confided in me that his son had always had a problem with what they considered an addiction to technology: he was glued to his computer and phone screen. With the stressors in his life requiring pacification, he dove even deeper into his addiction. These parents tried everything that they could think of to help their son out of what they perceived to be a simple "funk," but nothing worked. It was at this time that their own fears started to surface: they feared that their son wouldn't be able to "handle" his technology dependency, and they feared what all of this confusion and unrest revealed about them as parents. When there is a family member or someone very dear to us who is in crisis, despair tends to block solutions for a positive outcome, and instead creates a heaviness of thought and emotion. Distress rattles our attention and sends shock waves to our epicenter. Fear was at the heart of this matter for each member of this family.

To all problems there are multiple solutions; they need to be weighed and measured to elicit the best defense strategy. Once these parents understood and acknowledged what their son's vision for his life was, they were then able to design and schedule actions based on what would work best for their specific circumstances. My client and his spouse did not want these academic blunders to derail their son's future or their family's bond. For each of them, the goal was to learn valuable lessons from the past while building enduring character traits and developing a realistic path for advancement. With my support, they were able to create an agreement with their son that would balance his gaming tendencies with the importance of human interaction and scholarly progress. The "everything in moderation" strategy that we shaped gradually showed evidence of progress through small wins on a daily basis. His struggle with addiction would always be present, but as he made steady academic progress, it moved more into the background of his life rather than being in the driver's seat.

Fear is real. It is a powerful emotion. The feelings that surround fear can torment us. Fear can be from an old place, or it can be from a new angst. Our thoughts and feelings are not facts, even though they tend to have substantial sway over us. How we each carry our fear varies. Some of us have the ability to shed our fear as if we are casting aside a wet raincoat, while others hold onto it like a second skin and allow it to claim a spot in their body – the stomach, the head, or even the heart. In my professional capacity, I have seen fear stupefy far too many people in both their personal and professional lives.

The primary areas where fear lodges itself are: fear of failure, fear of embarrassment, fear of change, fear of uncertainty, fear of success, fear of responsibility, fear of making mistakes, and the fear of getting hurt. It is imperative that our fear does not hijack our potential for today and tomorrow. Our emotions power our motivation, so it is enormously helpful when we are able to gain freedom from our negative thoughts. Having courage does not mean that we are not afraid: it means that we are willing to step beyond our fear.

Experiencing fear is human. When we are grappling with our own demons, it is better to be in the driver's seat than in the passenger's seat: we need to acknowledge, respect, and own our fears. Those who are looking to ascend to their next level of success need to move beyond timid actions by first understanding what their deficiencies are, and then learning, practicing, and developing in those specific areas. Fears live in our head, but they are prohibitively potent in the ways that they can hold us back. Getting specific about what is actually freezing you up is an awareness that is critical to moving forward. If you are to heal, you will need to make peace with yourself and your situation. When you are able to be honest with yourself about what specifically is hampering your progress, you can begin to conquer your fears.

While I was in transit to a client meeting, I received an unexpected call from my client's husband letting me know that my client had just been in a very bad car accident. He went on to explain that her vehicle had been hit by a police officer's cruiser while the officer was responding to a call.

The law enforcement agent had a red light at the intersection. He did not have his emergency lights or siren active at the time of the motor vehicle impact. My client had a green light and was proceeding through the intersection when the collision happened. The primary responsibility of a police officer is to safeguard the public even when responding to a call. Instead, he had come barreling through the intersection at an incredible rate of speed that, upon investigation, revealed his skid marks being at least 30 feet long. The force that he hit her car with was so strong that her vehicle was propelled onto a neighboring street before she was able to finally gain enough control to bring it to a full stop. Two weeks after this intensely traumatic event, she received word from her insurance company that she was found to be 100% not at fault.

She knew from the force with which her head had hit the steering wheel that there would be repercussions. Unfortunately, the ER doctor at her local hospital didn't take the time to pursue the extent of her injuries, so she suffered in silence from a variety of symptoms without knowing what to attribute them to. Nightmares forced her to relive the trauma of the accident daily. She suffered from dizziness, frequent headaches, exhaustion, lack of appetite, and a general feeling of "fuzziness." Reading and writing emails became challenging for a woman who had been a creative writing major in college. The rental car sat in her driveway as she tried to conduct the majority of her business by phone. She chose not to mention any of these issues to anyone for fear of alarming her family and damaging her credibility in business. It took an episode of extreme dizziness followed by a fall down a flight of carpeted stairs before she came face to face with exactly what she was suffering from. Her husband was able to take her to the ER at one of Boston's world-class hospitals, where she was diagnosed with post-concussion syndrome. This diagnosis confirmed everything that she had been experiencing. She was referred to an orthopedist, a neurologist, and a psychotherapist. The orthopedist recommended surgery for her broken elbow followed by six to eight weeks of occupational therapy. The neurologist recommended a CT scan. The psychotherapist recommended that they "talk through" the accident on a weekly basis as a way to process through what had happened. She followed their recommendations verbatim.

From my client's perspective, things were moving at a snail's pace. The stress surrounding this terrifying event had created significant emotional turmoil in her recovery. Every aspect of her life seemed to require baby steps. She had been a road warrior who was accustomed to spending much of her day driving to meet with clients in person. For over four decades, she had been a top-producing outside sales professional. She had always prided herself on her independence and her boundless energy; now she was relegated to being dependent upon others for assistance with bathing, dressing, drying her hair, errands, food shopping, cooking, etc.

She told her husband that she wasn't sure she would ever be able to drive again. She told her colleagues that she wasn't sure if she would ever be able to work again. She told herself that she wasn't sure if she would ever get back to herself again. She perceived everything as a loss. These deep-seated fears kept her living in crisis. She didn't seem able to transition herself into living in recovery.

Her successful career and vibrant personal life had all been put on hold as she fought to get back to her baseline. My client had previously been one to prosper in spite of opposition, hardship, and any setbacks. When she was finally "sick and tired of being sick and tired," she knew that she was ready to begin her rebuilding process. She healed from her surgery, completed the full course of occupational therapy, physical therapy, and psychotherapy, and began taking strength training classes five days a week. She also began driving again, and slowly over a number of months she returned to her regular activities.

Even though we talked via phone on a number of occasions throughout her ordeal, there was a four-month hiatus before we were finally able to start working together again in person. I was curious about how she was able to come from such a dark place and ultimately accomplish all that she had. She told me that she believed that we each have our own relationship with fear. She knew that what had taken place for her the day of the accident had paralyzed her in fear. At some point in her recovery, she made a conscious decision to not allow fear to incapacitate her. She knew that she was willing to do whatever it took to get her life back. She hired a personal injury attorney to take on her case. This bold move was extremely difficult for her, but essential for her recovery. She believes her case is straightforward and will be settled easily. She doesn't expect that it will need to go to trial, but if it does she is ready to tell her story in a strong, clear voice.

Fear can haunt us. Some people's fears affect them so dramatically that tasks that were once interesting are now pure drudgery. We all have limitations, but they do not have to define us. Many people experience a gravitational pull on their behavior. Their lives are so fast-paced and over-stimulated that they are unable to centralize their thoughts. Ultimately, even relaxing becomes stressful because there is so much noise going on in their heads.

Our brains are wired to protect us. Taking chances is part of being alive. However, when the risk is escalated to against all odds, no two people respond in the same way. For some, fear tends to hinder and inhibit them, while for the bravest among us, it triggers a growth spurt, allowing us to aspire to a higher level of success. Open-mindedness helps us to be receptive to hearing fresh perspectives and learning new skills. Acquiring these assets, and then combining them with a heavy dose of endurance, enables us to fight through the many complexities we experience.

Don't give in to your Achilles heels. Fear can be so deeply embedded in the very essence of our being that we find ourselves on a laser-focused quest to avoid emotional pain and unhappiness. Prioritizing who you are, and more importantly, who you want to be, is critically important as you venture into a difficult journey of creating a brighter future. Having a visual of what you want for your life will help you through the most difficult times.

To reframe our perspective, we need to interrupt our habit loop by awakening the parts of our mind that desperately need a tune-up. To reverse ineffective habits and thoughts, spark your inner wisdom to support you in creating an avalanche of possibilities. Believe in yourself and you will be able to embrace a destiny where fear is no longer your co-pilot. The answers to all of your challenges are within you.

Your magic is what makes you tick: it is the essence of who you are, what you do, and how you do it. Accepting, confronting, and overpowering our darkest fears enables us to reveal a brighter side. Getting through the days of dread helps us to get to where happiness lives. Finding the joy in life again, and keeping it, has immeasurable value.

Top Nuggets of Wisdom

1 Fear stifles progress. Fear factors can be real or imagined. When there is genuine or perceived danger, pain, or threat, we have a tendency to display behaviors of fleeing, hiding, or freezing up.

2 Fear reaps havoc and fills our mind with stories of doubt and anxiety.

3 Remaining silent or ignoring problems can snowball into epic proportion – creating physical decay and degradation of motivation and inspiration to achieve.

PART 5

Stress

Stress is essential for survival. Any type of change, good or bad, is needed for progress. Positive or negative change can cause stress. Stress sensitivity varies between each one of us. Good stress can motivate and help us to accomplish milestones more efficiently. It can launch us onward to achieve more of our life's ambitions, ultimately leading us to a higher degree of happiness, success, and fulfillment. Problematic experiences cause distress and threaten our well-being. Stress can be caused by external sources, it can be self-generated, and sometimes it can even be a combination of the two. We experience all kinds of frequencies coming at us every second of every day. As a result, it is important to be deliberate with our comeback to stress, as it has a direct correlation to our counter-response. Perception of any situation can add to or reduce the stress load because our response to stressors is very individualized. Various situations can throw us off course; none of us can prevent stress from entering our lives. Stress is one of our body's natural defenses: it is vital for survival, especially when danger is lurking. Stress improves our abilities to respond to challenging or hazardous conditions. When stress kicks us into emergency mode, it can help us to react with a high degree of alertness.

Stress is a protective reaction. It is how our body and our mind respond to any kind of major or minor demand or threat. Universally experienced conditions such as pressure, strain, or tension are often associated with stress. We can actually "feel" stress because it affects most of us in both a psychological and a physical state of being that results from highly demanding or adverse circumstances. An actual or perceived challenge can give rise to a sense of fracture, often causing us to become agitated, anxious, depressed, isolated, irritable, overwhelmed, or unhappy.

A former client called me to help him through a full-fledged crisis situation between his business partner and himself. Sizing up the situation, I could see that the stress level was at full tilt. The chronic issues that they were having had reached an explosive state, creating a severely hostile environment throughout this multi-million-dollar company. He and his business partner were both charismatic, courageous, and self-confident. They both had innovative ideas and ambitious goals, and they pursued their aspirations with tenacity and with an urgent sense of purpose. Individually, dominant alphas can be dynamic and influential leaders, but having a partnership with two aggressively ego-fueled alphas can be a liability if not managed properly. When alpha tendencies like ambition, assertiveness, confidence, and competitiveness are taken too far or activated improperly, these legendary assets can turn into fatal flaws. This can create expensive problems for their company and wreak havoc on their employees, customers, and partnership. Even though they had a common thread of character traits, their leadership styles, their education, and their life experiences were distinctly different. Because they both felt that their way was the right way, there were many unreasonable expectations and unyielding opinions. Their viewpoints were dissimilar, and neither of them was willing to yield to the other for fear of displaying weakness. It is very difficult to make any traction when both parties are starting from a place of single-mindedness. When we are in crisis, we are not showing up as our best selves, which only inflames the problems. Unfortunately, there was too much damage that had been done between these two alphas and they could not make things work.

The majority of stressful situations unfold when significant changes take place that entail extra effort, new responsibilities, and a need for transformation. Change demands stepping into the unknown. Negative responses to challenges with change can have a detrimental influence on our health, our happiness, and the overall quality of our lives.

Our ability to handle distractions and pressures can change regularly based upon the many variables that occur during our day. Some of us get frazzled more easily and quickly than others, and often crumble due to the volume or complexities of our stressors. At times, it can simply be a minor bump in the road; however, when there are numerous bumps taking place simultaneously, that dynamic can exacerbate our level of stress. If or when we can uncloud the clutter in our minds, we can gain clarity. This opportunity allows us to realize that we are not at the mercy of our stressors. Learning what can positively and negatively influence our stress-overload levels is productive in reducing the damage that high levels of chronic stress can cause.

Stressful situations have a profound impact on our bodies. The most recognizable symptoms of stress are headaches, insomnia, back pain, neck pain, jaw pain, heartburn, nausea, nail-biting, fidgeting, stuttering, nervousness, anxiety, tardiness, trouble focusing, and a lack of interest towards endeavors that are typically of interest. Numerous people try to escape stressful situations by blocking them out of their mind or escaping by way of anything that makes them feel better. Oftentimes, this escape can take the form of a sudden shift in behavior and emotional tendencies towards addictive activities. Maintaining feelings of being overwhelmed over the long term have been known to undermine our mental and physical health. When we feel desperate, broken-hearted, envious, or enraged, it isn't an easy trek.

We all know people whose response to stress is to self-medicate with either drinking, drugging, gambling, cheating, or other behaviors that show a lack of self-control. These ways of calming our nerves to relieve emotional anguish will not eliminate stress and will only make matters worse. When you are inordinately stressed, it is critical to watch for the signs that represent "crash and burn" so that you can implement positive remedial strategies to decompress. In extreme cases, when we are consistently overloaded and struggling to cope with demands, chronic stress can manifest itself in many ways including violent actions, suicide, stroke, and heart attack.

One of the most stressful times is the holiday season. Emotionally charged expectations and assumptions are at the core of why stress is so intense during the holidays. It starts for most of us with a baseline of having already busy lives, and then layering onto that an over-extended schedule that comprises entertaining, shopping, and traveling. Next, we layer on complex family situations that may include divorce, death, illness, and/or addiction. It is a recipe made for a pressure cooker!

Every family has its own unique set of baggage and no family is exempt. Family constellations can cause holiday regression, especially when tense situations escalate. Family stress becomes extra potent during these times. We can't go back in time to undo childhood anguish; however, we can be mindful of our emotions at the holidays so as not to add additional stress into our lives and the lives of those we care about. If we can rationally and maturely focus on the present day as opposed to dredging up the dysfunctional behaviors of the past, we will be able to capture a healthy and more productive approach to successfully managing stress during the holiday season.

You may be one of the lucky ones who doesn't succumb to holiday stress. If that is the case, I would venture to guess that you have other complicated stressors. It is important to give yourself the time that you need to process through whatever it is that is "maxing you out." It may be an upcoming family event, a speech that you will be delivering next week, or a promotion that you are in line for. No matter how stressful your life seems, there are always strides that you can make to relieve some pressure and gain control in a productive way. Knowing that you innately have the capacity to self-manage your lifestyle, your thoughts, your emotions, and the way that you deal with problems allows you to bridle stress rather than succumbing to having stress bridle you.

Top Nuggets of Wisdom

1 Stress is universally experienced. It is a real or perceived challenge or threat that can give rise to a sense of fracture – often causing us to become agitated, anxious, depressed, isolated, irritable, overwhelmed, or unhappy.

2 Stress is essential for survival. Any type of change, good or bad, is needed for progress. Positive or negative change can cause stress.

3 Stress sensitivity varies between each one of us. Stress can be caused by external sources or it can be self-generated. Sometimes it can even be a combination of the two.

CHAPTER 8

Relationships

The state of being connected to others can have the greatest significance in our lives. These "connections" can be in the form of friendship, family, love interest, or work colleague, along with a variety of community relationships within our society. The way we think and behave towards each other will never be perfect. What one person considers happiness might be agitating or irritating to someone else. It is key to ground your views of happiness by your own expectations.

Robust relationships enrich our lives, whereas dicey relationships can cause emotional pain and sometimes even physical harm. Every single relationship goes through various degrees of stressful times. Even the healthiest of relationships require ongoing physical and mental effort, usually in the form of mutual concessions and compromises.

There is no magic potion for successful relationships; however, the most functional relationships don't sweat the small stuff. Fairness to each other is a key ingredient in making and maintaining a solid bond. All relationships need to be cultivated and cared for, though not all relationships are meant to last forever. Glancing back over our life story, we can recognize those who have remained long-term contacts, while also appreciating those who were merely transient. It can be difficult to look back and think about those who we cared so deeply about who are now living totally separate lives from ours. They were people who once were such an important part of our lives, who provided unique experiences and a sense of comfort during various stages of our lives. As life continues onward, it is worthwhile to take the time to gain a deeper understanding and appreciation for the experiences we share with people while they are in our lives.

Fostering supportive connections takes time. Healthy relationships have a number of essential elements to them including mutual admiration, respect, honesty, trustworthiness, loyalty, dependability, empathy, non-judgmentalism, and transparent communication. It is just as important to recognize what a healthy relationship looks like as it is to be able to identify an unhealthy one. The red flags of a relationship spiraling out of control could include, but are not limited to, tactics such as manipulation, deceptiveness, selfishness, lying, hiding unhealthy habits, controlling, criticizing; being verbally, physically, emotionally, or financially abusive; harassment, unsubstantiated blame, jealousy, anger, resentment, unhealthy competition, codependency; lack of trust, respect, support, empathy, or dependability. Over time, these destructive personalities create a poisonous atmosphere that can become the status quo and then become accepted as the new normal.

During all ages and all phases of our lives, we will have "happy-day friends." These opportunistic people disguise themselves as friends. They don't have the true loyalty, support, or genuineness of a real friend. There is very little, if any, reciprocity from them. They are temporary in our lives even though they may act as if they are permanent fixtures in the role of best friend for a period of time. These people "Velcro" themselves to us. This style of person oftentimes clings to those who are overachievers to be able to live vicariously through them, gaining pleasure in doing so. Some even make it a hobby to befriend others who they admire so that they can picture themselves in the other person's life. These happy-day friends are leeches who are interested in your possessions such as your sports or luxury car(s), your recreational vehicle(s), your elegant home, your vacation property, your high-end clothing (that they can borrow), your network, and your status.

Happy-day friends have "vacancy defects": when grueling or unpleasant times move in – they move on. Many people believe that the bonds of friendship should transcend the highs and lows of life, similarly to the taking of marriage vows. The reality is that people come into our lives and leave for reasons of fate or choice. The speed and demands of our world have compromised the quality of relationships. Most individuals don't mean to be callous, but they are overwhelmed by their own circumstances. Opportunistic individuals are around us for a specific reason. Once their needs are met, they usually vacate the relationship and look for someone else who can accommodate their unmet needs or wants. When we rely upon the achievements of others to help us feel alive, it can slowly erode our own aspirations and our beliefs in our own competencies. Be the leader of your own life by leveling up your own experiences instead of living through the stolen lens of other people's triumphs.

Every healthy relationship requires that the people involved are independently whole. There is a difference between being someone's priority and being someone's everything. It is detrimental to be someone's everything. Not only is it a tremendous amount of pressure, but it is not beneficial for one person to be our world. Getting caught up in the honeymoon phase of any new relationship is one thing, but having the awareness to realize that this phase isn't sustainable is another. It is a vulnerable place for any adult to be inordinately dependent upon another human being. Too much of anyone or anything is an imbalance that will not serve us well in the long run. We each need our own oxygen – our own true identity. We should strive to make our own unique and individual contributions to this world.

When one partner attempts and ultimately succeeds in exerting control and power over the other partner, be it physically, sexually, and/or emotionally, the relationship has crossed over into an unwholesome and harmful state. Just as healthy relationships have distinct similarities, so do sickly ones. If you feel pressure to change who you are, if you need to justify your innocent actions, if you are being blamed for your partner's shortcomings, if arguments are not being settled fairly, if you are experiencing feelings of distress on a regular basis, if your usual self-confidence has plummeted, equality is clearly lacking in your relationship and it could become injurious to your health.

Only you know how extreme the situation is, so it needs to be your decision alone if you stay or if you go. If the situation honestly hasn't reached a toxic level, and if both people are committed to making the necessary changes, you may be able to remedy the adverse conditions in your relationship to benefit both of you. However, if it has become contaminated such that there are actions causing emotional or physical aggression, cruelty, injury, or trauma, those are clear signs that the relationship is abusive. If that is the case, you should strongly consider getting help and ending that connection. Releasing yourself from a dangerous liaison can seem impossible if you are the one who has been repeatedly mistreated because it has become your new normal. Those who have allowed themselves to be mistreated often stay in these relationships because they feel embarrassed, guilty, helpless, or even worried about how others will judge them. They may be afraid of what might happen if they leave. Others stay for prolonged periods because they are wishing and hoping that their abuser will change. Whether it is a friendship, a romance, a work relationship, or some other type of relationship we find ourselves engaged in, we can't make another person want to change. When we desire their change more than they do, it rarely turns out the way we want it to.

The daughter of a good friend of mine graduated three years ago with top honors from an Ivy League college. Her career path was wide open, and employers were standing in line to recruit her. She decided to go with a well-known global technology firm because they offered her a management position right from the start. From the outside looking in, it appeared that my friend's daughter had it all because she had made incredible strides in her career in such a short period of time. The part of her life where she had not been successful was in her love life, but it looked like her luck was starting to change. She had connected with "a great guy" through social media. This "great guy" was a friend of a friend, so it seemed above board to make the initial connection virtually. They found that they had a number of acquaintances in common, and that they had even played the same sport for a number of years. Over the next few months, things continued to go extremely well through their social media conversations, so they decided to take a great leap of faith and meet in person. The attraction was instantaneous. It seemed to be a case of love at first sight. They started dating. For the first few months, everything was "magical." They both claimed to have never experienced anything like this in any of their prior relationships. She felt as if he understood her, and he said that she "got him" more than anyone else he had ever met. Their close bond seemed to be special. About four months into the relationship, things between them started getting bumpy. The intense connection began to dissipate. She wasn't quite sure what had happened, but she was no fool: she recognized that things had changed dramatically. She was a "silver lining" kind of a person, but in just a few short weeks his behavior had put her on a rollercoaster ride that took her from joyful and bubbly to shattered and heartbroken. It had become clear that he had some significant gremlins. She tried to support him through his difficulties, but it came back to bite her emotionally. He erupted when his career demands were high and he couldn't produce solid results. He exploded when he had intense financial pressures with less than anticipated outcomes. While he appeared to be an untroubled and highly successful guy, it was all a façade. He became cruel. He became verbally and emotionally abusive. He drank excessively. He became unpredictable. He was no longer a man of his word. When he eventually developed a skin hunger for shallow girls, she knew that she had to leave him. He had so much noise in his head that he was only capable of living a subpar life. His actions were not signs of love. His behavior had sabotaged any chance for them to have a future together.

Those closest to her were perplexed that she was in such a toxic relationship. They couldn't figure out why she would settle for such an outwardly aggressive partner in her personal life when she had such solid self-esteem in her professional life. She knew that she had gotten caught up in the initial magic of the relationship and had temporarily lost her way. She realized that his poisonous baggage had held hostage a huge amount of her time along with her energy and her emotions. When she had reached her threshold for being his emotional and verbal punching bag, she made the commitment to herself to never again be with someone who she couldn't trust. Because of her career trajectory, she was able to leverage her business skills to support her in making this tough decision. Once she had gained clarity and found her inner strength again, her ever-reliable smart thinking provided her with the best path forward. She chose to step up, step out, and move on as the leader of her own life. She shed many tears as she went through the various stages of grief, but gradually her heartache became less all-consuming. It has been far from an easy trek, but she was able to redirect her energy to heal herself. The hardship she slogged through and the wisdom she gained provided her with a template of what she will and won't permit in a romantic relationship in her future.

It is during extreme times when we often discover our true character and the true character of others. Many times, fatal flaws in one's character can shipwreck a relationship. Being the leaders of our own lives means that we need to recognize the dysfunction and break away from these types of toxic relationships for a healthier destiny. Interpersonal experiences leave a lasting imprint on us. Those coming out of unhealthy relationships can experience low self-esteem. They may feel incredibly unprotected on their own. These poisonous experiences impact how we develop and how we behave in future human interactions. Failures that tug at our heartstrings are often the source of abundant psychological anguish no matter what age we are.

When we wake up to the realization that either our mind, our body, or our soul has been jeopardized, it's time to create a healthier tomorrow. Engaging with a trusted support system is essential. Rebuild or construct a solid foundation of wholesome relationships – a core group of people who you "know, like, and trust." Creating this type of multilevel platform of strength radiates an emotional life support system that unconditionally listens, encourages, inspires, and challenges those in its orbit. Invigorating those bonds provides a safety net for life's biggest challenges, empowering us with the real courage and confidence to go out into the world and make our dreams a reality.

Significant relationships are built and maintained when there is a connection of common interest, understanding, and mutual benefit. To accelerate leadership development, more focus needs to be put on recognizing the power of forging meaningful relationships through mutual trust. There is a difference between the power *of* a relationship and the power *in* a relationship. In healthy relationships, the decision-making of a power structure is fluid, as it changes based upon the specifics of how the relationship adapts to new circumstances and tackles new challenges.

The power of a relationship is about helping each other succeed. The inspirational influencing in trusting relationships favorably affects and effects concepts, behaviors, and actions. Intentional leaders gain this type of connection with others through formal and informal networks. Relational leadership can be done by anyone – not just those with a leadership title.

Genuine leaders continue to learn and grow throughout their lifetime. They nurture the requisite skills and abilities that will galvanize the support of key participants so that they can build formidable networks. They awaken and energize collaboration and amazing outgrowths with their inspiring and empowering talents.

As leaders, we need to create and maintain a workforce that feels valued: one that is engaged and productive. When we devote the right amount of time and attention to protect and celebrate our valuable resources, they will prosper.

A business friend of mine was contemplating stepping off the ledge of "big business" into the unknown without any safety net. This would be unsettling for even the bravest of us. Having spent seventeen years with two of the nation's largest investment firms, she had learned quite well how to weigh and measure a lot of different pluses and minuses for her clients. She used this same protocol for herself and ultimately made the calculated decision that it was time to listen to her gut and venture out on her own. She was forward thinking and strategically intentional about combining an impressive, diverse brain power of a string of stars – her business partners and their leadership team. The combined competencies of this exceptional team were nothing short of awe-inspiring. Making good decisions from "go" created a solid foundation from the start. They positioned their market niche carefully. They had strong individual brand recognition and extensive meaningful connections. The norms of reciprocity with social capital are something that this firm valued and put much attention towards. The team's social network was the reason for the firm's instant success and continuous growth. Their collaborative relations allowed for a number of great opportunities to rapidly grow its health.

My business friend was a consummate entrepreneur, so she knew that she could be structuring a lethal combination when she brought together a team comprising "center of the universe" superstar egos. A team of people who believe that they are "important" could be a huge barrier for working effectively together. Often these types of personalities put their own agendas and their own gratification ahead of others. I've witnessed this situation firsthand and it erodes the effectiveness of the organization as a whole. Overactive egos give people a distorted view of their self-importance. This dynamo team could have easily become hyper-competitive, which would have resulted in highly aggressive, counterproductive behavior. My friend made a point of keeping this topic front and center in their everyday world so that it didn't become a fatal flaw for this new firm. It is imperative for leaders to be able to collaborate with their eyes wide open. This allowed for more effective communication and better alignment with objectives and goals, creating enhanced individual as well as combined accomplishments.

These superstars realized that they needed to work together to think through the best ideas, otherwise nothing productive would get accomplished. This dream team was able to surpass its five-year aspirations within the first six months of the new business being established.

It goes without saying that real success cannot be obtained without the capacity to leverage extraordinary professional and personal relationships. No one does it alone. Building and nurturing robust relationships in all aspects of our lives frequently leads to successful outcomes. We are social beings and maintaining healthy relationships is essential for how we each function within society. The common thread for the most successful businesses, whether they are a start-up or a large international organization, is the human beings behind the name of the business. Investing in a high-quality team, rather than pivoting to the best idea, will lead us to the greatest outcomes.

Top Nuggets of Wisdom

1 The state of being connected to others can have the greatest significance in our lives.

2 Every relationship has varying degrees of stressful times. Even the healthiest of relationships take ongoing physical and mental effort including mutual concessions and compromises.

3 There is no magic potion for successful relationships. However, the most functional relationships don't sweat the small stuff. They are built on trust, mutual respect, and compatibility.

CHAPTER 9

Betrayal

In order to have a more thriving life, it is important to focus our interactions on people who we trust and who we have an affinity with. Trust provides a feeling of comfort and is at the heart of any healthy relationship, be it personal or professional. Trust, or the lack thereof, permeates every type of relationship. When our trust is fractured, we are left feeling shocked, angry, fearful, and hurt. Betrayal can shake us to our core. Alliances collapse under the weight of implicit or explicit betrayal. When deceit and denial are used to conceal a transgression, it causes even more destruction than the infringement itself. Disloyalty can be towards a person, an organization, or even a country. Oftentimes, the greater the trust one has with another, the more significant an impact the betrayal has upon us.

Betrayal jolts and erodes the integrity of a relationship to its marrow. Self-interest types are super-saturated in themselves so that their insensitivities have the power to impair others. These people gain satisfaction by stirring up trouble; they get enjoyment out of manipulating others. What they are often not aware of is that betrayal is both a personal and a professional weakness. It is frequently associated with an unrestrained desire for excessive achievement. It shows up as being deliberately hurtful or careless towards others, which comes from their own limited capacity for self-awareness.

A few years ago, a top performer that worked at a manufacturing company hired me to support her with a difficult situation at her office. The company she was working for was struggling financially. It was clear to her that the lack of growth in the business was because of the consistently low customer satisfaction scores. In the three years that she had worked there, the process flow had become overly cumbersome. As new products and services were added to the company's platform, it only exacerbated the problems. No one had ever taken a thorough and measured approach as to what it would take to enhance the process flow. Management's tunnel vision had created a tangled web of challenges.

My client would regularly update her manager on the obstacles that the company as a whole was facing, but he said that it wasn't his problem, and that he couldn't be bothered due to his overflowing workload. My client was very frustrated with her manager's response because her past experiences had provided her with a keen eye for uncovering and cleaning up areas of inefficiency. After many conversations that we had together, and with her not being able to sit on the sidelines, she again went to her manager with an idea to activate a major process improvement initiative that would significantly reduce the root cause of their customers' complaints. Her manager reluctantly agreed to her undertaking of this enterprise if she stayed on top of all of her regular responsibilities. She agreed, and for the next twelve months she did both. It was exhausting, but she felt that it was well worth the effort. She could visualize the value that this would have for the company and its customers. Several of her colleagues were also passionate about the many streamlining efficiencies and total cycle time reduction.

Since this was an over-and-above effort for everyone on the team, as they too had their regular work to do, the changes took much longer than they would have liked. They discovered that there were outsourced delays, inventory control inefficiencies, lack of consistency in quality, process flow challenges, and point of contact issues. In addition, there were major obstacles with prioritizing dealer orders over consumer orders, which caused huge shipping delays for the end consumer. Manufacturing was rewarded by the volume of production each day versus ensuring that the correct manufacturing workflow was followed. Out of respect, even though her manager was lukewarm at best with this effort, she provided him with updates on a regular basis. Finally, the process improvement team was at a point where they had identified and resolved all of the issues. They were ready to go live with all the enhancements. It was a thrilling time for the entire team.

What she didn't know was that her boss had been, behind the scenes, sharing with the executives "his ideas" and "his efforts" to lead this process improvement. While my client was out of the office on an approved day off, he had scheduled a meeting with the executives to officially launch the new process. He took full credit for the extensive work that my client had put in without even mentioning that she had played an integral part in identifying the issues, and in leading, and then launching, this overhaul to completion. The news of his deception caught her completely off guard. She was speechless as she had no inkling of his sabotaging activities. While his lack of character angered her greatly, his actions paralyzed her. In an instant, he had stripped her of all trust, loyalty, and commitment, all of which she had firmly possessed just moments before the shock.

Initially, she had been unable to rally as she had immersed herself in an emotionally toxic space. Once we talked through the situation and she had mustered up the courage, she decided she was ready to speak up. His lack of integrity, dishonesty, and immoral behavior was well beyond anything that she had ever experienced. She felt that it was important to directly convey to her boss the disappointment, hurt, and anger that she was experiencing due to his pathological web of deceit. It was important to my client to be able to articulate her view, yet not compromise her character, so she calmly asked her manager why he had taken credit for her work and launched the new process without her. He shot back at her that her work was his work because she worked for him. He said that he had every right to have the meeting and share the new process with the executives without her being there. Despite her being a seasoned professional, having the rug pulled out from underneath her like that, left her feeling insecure, untrusting, and immediately disengaged from her job, her boss, and the company as a whole. She and her colleagues had worked diligently, and collectively they were thrilled to see this major process improvement launch. Her boss had taken advantage of their efforts and leveraged it for his own advancement. She had lost all respect for her manager.

My client was no longer going to let him take credit for any of her work. She was done. In a little over a week's time, not only had I supported her in giving her notice, but she had quickly secured an excellent career change that she was very excited about. When she walked out of the company's doors for the last time, she told me she felt a rush of fresh air and sunshine. Leaving the company and her colleagues hadn't been easy, but she had done what she needed to do. She had been blindsided, but she hadn't turned a blind eye. Throughout the emotional betrayal of trust, she had stayed true to herself.

People's extreme ambition, greed, or desperation can dominate their conduct to such a degree that they don't do the right thing. Excessive ambition can inflict harm on careers, organizations, and colleagues. Overly ambitious individuals often overstep their bounds. Steamrolling over others is not a sustainable way to climb the ladder of success. When our ambition shows up as success-mania, it becomes counterproductive and self-destructive. It is not easy, but it is very valuable to treasure our hard-learned lessons in order to be able to move forward in a decisive direction. While many instances of betrayal can take place from a higher rung in management towards a lower rung in the employee food chain, sometimes trust can be busted by a new hire.

My client, a senior manager in corporate America, had an open position for a junior-level person with a job description requiring skills beyond those of an entry-level employee. My client received a resume and a strong cover letter from a freshly minted college graduate who didn't have the requisite skills, but who reminded my client of herself when she was just starting out. My client talked with human resources to have this candidate come in for a professional discussion to determine if she had the capacity to function at a junior level if my client had the time to mentor her. Human resources had already identified a number of solid candidates who were turn-key for the position, but my client went out on a limb to hire this young woman and thereby give her not only the opportunity to sharpen her skills, but also the opening to help ease her path forward in her career.

I remember the day that my client called me in a panic. A number of her colleagues had started coming to her to share that the new hire had been trying to sabotage my client's personal brand, making my client look bad while making herself look better. At first, my client was in disbelief, but as the number of people coming to her increased, she felt stabbed in the back. She was crushed. My client had mentioned to me on a number of occasions how she had regularly let the new hire know that her efforts were valued and appreciated, she had provided the new hire with opportunities to advance in her job responsibilities, and the new hire was well compensated. To my client, everything was going extremely well. In reality, the new hire had been intentionally misleading and deceiving my client.

As much as retaliation might have made my client feel better in the short run, our work together enabled her to understand that it would not serve her well in the long run. Instead of having a knee-jerk response, my client kept her emotions in check and tried to be open-minded. She took the time to self-reflect and see if there could be a deeper meaning behind the new hire's actions. My client needed time to ruminate on the facts and size up the situation before responding. Quickly, it became clear to my client that the new hire was intentionally defaming and alienating my client from both management and her co-workers due to her excessive ambition.

Backstabbing is a betrayal that leaves scars. Backstabbers are often motivated by delusional beliefs that the only way to get ahead and to stay ahead is to stomp on others. The new hire sought self-promotion rather than embracing and nurturing a trusting, supportive culture. My client was astounded as to how this employee could have betrayed her in such a narcissistic way. I shared with my client the need to anchor her recovery by choosing to take actions that aligned with her personal values as well as the company's deep-rooted culture and well-established brand. I encouraged her to be true to her inner self, knowing that she would be able to make her best decisions from there. She needed to rise above the dishonesty and the deception that she had been subjected to. By embracing a higher-path response, she showed up as a powerful role model for her team. My client resisted the urge to stoop to the new hire's level. The less than favorable habits of undermining and sabotaging really spoke to the new hire's own insecurities and character flaws. I explained to my client that it was best to confront the shifty behavior as soon as possible because avoidance would only exacerbate the issue. Oftentimes, betrayers fail to fully grasp the negative consequences that their behaviors have on others or on themselves from a credibility and respectability perspective. My client confronted the new hire calmly yet firmly, explaining that she was aware of her unethical actions and that she was very disappointed in her lack of integrity. My client went on to say that she expected a higher caliber of conduct from the new hire, especially after everything that my client had done to support her growth and development. I continued to work with my client to get her to a point where she could rise up again to be the leader that she had been before this humiliating episode had unfolded. I explained to my client that it was important that she be able to move on or it would inevitably spill over into other aspects of her professional as well as her personal life. The new hire continued with her sabotaging ways and was terminated due to her ongoing violation of company policy.

We have all experienced the sting of deceit – we cannot prevent betrayal. Deceptive actions range in magnitude from mild to extreme. The bigger the betrayal, the more considerable the impact and the more challenging it is to come to terms with it. I do not believe that we all need to figure out the reasons for the bad behavior in order for us to process through to a healthier place. People behave without scruples for a variety of reasons, many of which have nothing to do with us. Allowing ourselves to get caught up in the vortex of why they did what they did is not productive. Recovery requires that we let go if we are to move forward towards an improved destiny.

Betrayal is omnipresent not just in our work lives, but in our personal lives as well. One of the most ruinous examples of betrayal is infidelity. Infidelity oftentimes plants its roots in people who have a basic crisis with their own self-esteem. In some cases, they may lack real empathy, they may be excessively self-serving, or they may be used to getting their own way. Sometimes, they may have addictive tendencies. At the same time, they may be insecure and disoriented because they see themselves as too fat, too short, too bald, or too old.

The decision to become a cheater doesn't happen overnight. Most people believe that they will never be cheated on. However, with widespread and unrestricted access to the internet, it is easier now for people to break their marriage vows than at any other time in our history. For some people, infidelity takes place if a spouse has sex with someone else. For other people, infidelity takes place if a spouse is emotionally involved with someone else even though no sex is involved. In order for a relationship to truly work, there must be a foundational blend of trust, honesty, respect, and effective communication. Both partners must feel safe in the knowledge that the promises they made to each other won't be broken.

A client of mine that I've known personally for a number of years is in the process of divorcing her husband of more than 35 years. The dissolution of their marriage paralyzed her and shocked their tight group of friends to the core. In their social circle, they seemed to be "that couple." They had a beautiful home, two wonderful grown children, careers that they loved, and interesting vacations that they took; and they were both very active in their community. When people were with them, the conversation flowed easily because they were always supportive of each other and never had an unkind word to say about one another. Their life appeared to be as close to perfect as anyone could imagine. Everyone who knew them wondered what had gone so horribly wrong. Having been married for just shy of 30 years myself, I have a realistic view that all marriages have their ups and downs, with some years having more than their fair share of downs and other years where the ups have been plentiful. In my client's case, it wasn't so much the ups as it was the downs which caused her professional career to faulter. At times, we were talking on a daily basis just to help her get through the day. It was a struggle to stay focused on her business goals and objectives when her personal life was unexpectedly being turned upside down.

My client's husband had two distinct sides to his personality; he was not bipolar, but his behavior certainly was. He was living two markedly separate lives. While his public face was always one of warmth and affability, his dark side was that he was glued to the internet seeking out more and more risky affairs. The women he selected were highly sexual, but also highly unstable. As his desires became more and more insatiable over time, he became less and less discreet in his desire to cover his tracks. Things exploded when one of the women sent a letter to his wife detailing the explicit details of the affair that she was having with my client's husband. This woman had no conscience; she even recounted intimate word-for-word conversations that my friend and her husband had shared with each other and which my client's husband had in turn shared with this woman. The betrayal that my client experienced was beyond anything she could have imagined. It pushed her into a deep depression that took the better part of twelve months to crawl out from under. It has been a slow and gradual healing process. She still feels the sting of deceit, but she is focusing on the positives that she has in her life and she is starting to gain excitement for what the future holds for her.

Every tale of woe has its own story. All setbacks require time for essential healing to take place. When there is a violation of trust in any relationship, that betrayal can cause a distressing amount of emotional trauma. The negative frame of mind and rollercoaster of emotions that often accompany betrayal can be painful and difficult to recover from. When deceit rears its ugly head, our fortitude takes a powerful punch. When our trust has been compromised, fear gets in the way of trusting again. There are no guarantees when it comes to human dynamics. Trusting someone is a decision you must make for yourself. There is no magic moment that allows us to trust again. One individual's poor behavior is not a reflection of how others will treat you. The negative actions of others do not mean that you have to own that victim mentality. Everyone is afraid of something. Mental toughness helps us to abate our fears along the way. We all have hurdles. Past wrongs or present injustices need not define you. The victim mentality does not serve you well. You can carve out a more advantageous path forward with self-compassion as your cornerstone. It is far from easy, but I would encourage you to be more intentional about replacing those negative emotions with upbeat, more proactive thoughts which will assist you in regaining the stability that is often lost with betrayal. Our true strength emerges when we can free ourselves from hurt and anger and reposition our mindset to remain true to our values and beliefs. Break free and reclaim your life by leaving behind those who do not have the same baseline of character as you do. Move forward with a "can do" mindset. As the leader of your own life, empower the wherewithal to trust again. Focus your energy on making traction in the direction that serves you best.

Top Nuggets of Wisdom

1 Trust, or the lack thereof, permeates every type of relationship, be it personal or professional. In order to have a more thriving life, it is important to focus our interactions on people who we trust and who we have an affinity with.

2 When our trust is fractured, we are left feeling shocked, angry, fearful, and hurt. Betrayal can shake people to their core. Alliances collapse under the weight of implicit or explicit betrayal.

3 When deceit and denial are used to conceal a transgression, it causes even more destruction than the infringement itself. Oftentimes, the greater the trust one has with another, the more significant an impact the betrayal has upon us.

CHAPTER 10

Showing Up

Perception is reality. The attitudes we project and the words that we speak, along with the body language we exude, can be a game changer in a positive or a negative way. We alone are responsible for our public persona. Our ethics and our values characterize who we are. As human beings, our consciousness is based upon how we see ourselves; our experiences are perceived through our own eyes, our own brain, and our own senses. We all need to have some self-centeredness, or we have no sense of self. However, when there is a distinct underbelly of excessive concentration solely on our own well-being, that usually attunes with a lack of consideration for others and enables us to show up as egocentric.

Others don't see what we see when we look in the mirror. We think we know how people perceive us when in actuality we really don't. Our social behaviors can come across differently than we imagine.

Negative energy can be ingrained within us without us even realizing it. Negativity breeds and attracts more negativity. There is a difference between constantly radiating negative energy and being realistic about the pros and cons of life.

I worked with a client who always focused on what everyone else was doing wrong. These wrongdoings were from her perspective, without any insight into what was truly going on with those individuals who she criticized. Her behavior created an exhausting cloud of drama for everyone around her. She did not realize that she was hijacking her own progress by being unremitting in finding faults in others. She preferred moaning and groaning about other people's slips in conduct instead of acknowledging and addressing her own demons. In her world view, all problems were caused by others because she was always being wronged by someone other than herself. She displayed histrionics with every hiccup of a challenge. She was so hyper-focused on her own stressors that she didn't realize how tightly she was wound around playing the blame game.

The irony of this situation was that she was a kind-hearted person who was just clueless as to how she was showing up. Her obsession with finding fault with others was holding her hostage from the direction that she really wanted to go in for her own life. Her interactions in all aspects of her life were emotionally noxious. Though she believed that everyone respected her, she was visionless in this regard. To improve relationships, I encouraged her to lead with her eyes wide open. Part of that journey was to first realize what she was doing and to then start making the necessary traction to improve her quality of life. I was asking her to realize the error of her ways, but it was the only style of living that she had ever known. It was painful for her to accept how truly lost she had become. After many months of working together, she was able to accept that she had an adverse disposition that was deficient in genuine warmth and appreciation. Once she was able to face the music, she became committed to making the essential changes in her demeanor. This required her to gain awareness of when she was attracting the wrong situations and the wrong people into her life. Simultaneously, she also needed to gain a degree of introspection so that she would be able to observe firsthand how her mind immediately went to a negative thought with every situation she encountered. Gaining the strength to transition her defeatist thoughts continues to be a rough slog for her. With a refurbished sense of personal integrity, she continues to focus on better aligning her words with her actions. Caring about creating harmony is now her new normal. I am proud of her dedication to creating a better life. Amazing progress can happen when we have a solid commitment that we can fuse together with determination. She knows without question that she needs to stay the course. It takes time to change a lifetime of bad habits, but she is making slow yet steady progress. I believe in her and I know that she has what it takes inside of her to make it happen.

The dynamics associated with each of our lives varies. Some of us are not as hard boiled as others are to appreciate and persevere through the stormiest of times. When the situation becomes extremely difficult, those who are emotionally stronger understand the need to calm themselves down so that they can hyper-focus to assess both the situation and the best possible outcomes. This happens when we are able to dig deeper and work harder to overcome the threat or challenge.

During the 122nd Boston Marathon, the weather was absolutely brutal, with hypothermic extreme temperatures, torrential rain with flash flood warnings, and relentless headwinds of over 40 mph. The weather was punishing for volunteers, medical staff, public safety personnel and fans; and the most impacted were the over 25,000 runners that actually completed the race. The "survival of the fittest" tendencies were quite noticeable. The misery index was beyond anything that most of these runners had ever experienced. During every aspect of the race, the commitment, the contagious energy, and the smiling faces of the volunteers and support staff were inspiring.

Pressure to perform under such extreme conditions, coupled with a dose of self-doubt, became a recipe for some runners who never made it out of the athletes' village in Hopkinton, Massachusetts, while others were able to hunker down and surge through with an all-out determination to cross the finish line.

Whether we are running a marathon during extreme conditions, or looking to expand our career, how we show up makes a difference in determining the end products of our lives. Stretching ourselves with honesty and intentionality will help us to continue to evolve as the leaders of our own lives both personally and professionally.

A CEO asked if I would work with him as he transitioned into a new career opportunity. I was initially hesitant because the "word on the street" about him was not favorable. My criteria for working with any client is that they have to be committed and open-minded to accelerate their success. Over the years, I have learned and have achieved more optimal results when I form my own views versus judging someone on the views of others. I do not put a lot of weight on what others think of a person or a situation: I lead with what I experience firsthand.

Sadly, my own experiences with this client confirmed the word on the street. I had known him for over a year, and the few times that we had interacted I was left with the feeling that he thought that he was superior to most people in intelligence, power, wealth, talent, and his place in society. I believe his elitism started when he was a young boy and then continued to be fostered well into adulthood until he eventually became a narcissist. His bad reputation required damage control.

This senior leader's pompous style was a turnoff to many, and yet he had no concept that he had snobbish behavior. We don't know what we don't know. When we are raised a certain way, we grow up with our own definition of what is "normal" behavior, and yet the "normal" barometer indicates something different to every one of us. His haughty approach made others doubt their own self-worth. "Showing up" this way can ding one's reputation and one's personal brand, and eventually it will limit one's overall success.

I have always tried to meet people where they are. In our one-to-one sessions, I had the opportunity to see a totally different side of this client, a side that was quite pleasant. I found myself looking forward to and eventually enjoying our time together. Often elitists are harboring feelings of deep insecurity themselves, but since I had observed both sides of his style, I was able to bring attention to, and then help him to understand, how he was being perceived. This revelation was a bona fide shock to him – I believe he genuinely had no idea. Through our work together, he learned to embrace and reveal his genuine self to others. This has elevated his relationships with authenticity. On a number of occasions, he has turned negative relationships into more approving ones because he is leading his life and showing up with a more approachable style.

To build relationships with lasting impact requires that our motives be upstanding. Spotlight your curiosity to learn new ideas and foster collaborative, long-lasting relationships. Surround yourself with those who have similar guiding principles to create a more robust and authentic lifestyle. For the most successful outcomes, build and manage your life in a way that expands your universe of opportunities by consistently reinforcing your reputation as a genuine giver. Those who are the takers in our world cannot sustain the test of time. Those who are fakers are found out sooner rather than later.

People tend to be more generous in their personal lives while concurrently having sharp elbows in their careers. I believe it is because the competitive nature of business brings out a different side in each of us. Showing up as your genuine self is freeing. People want to see the true essence of who you are every day. Oftentimes, people carefully craft a persona that they think others want them to have. They hide their faults so that no one sees the real them. As human beings, we long to be liked, imperfections and all. Be brave and embrace your vulnerabilities. Once we make the decision to become our whole selves, we can start to accept others as their whole selves.

Our comments and our actions are observed and digested by those who we know and even those who we do not. I challenge you to ask more than one person who knows you well how they would describe you to someone else. Try to keep an open mind and remember to show gratitude for their honesty even though their feedback may be hard to digest. Allow yourself the opportunity to let everything you have heard sink in, and then be brutally honest with yourself. See if you can uncover common themes from the feedback you receive. Sometimes we are pleasantly surprised by what people say about us; other times we are taken aback. It is just as important to celebrate your first-class character traits as it is to identify where you need to expand your focus to be your inimitable future self.

A C-suite executive who I had worked with previously referred a business friend of his to me. After our initial discussion, I customized a statement of the work that would best support his needs. I then provided him with a formal written proposal based on our agreed-upon discussion. In the weeks that followed, it was "radio silence." I had reached out to him about half a dozen times over a few months by email as well as leaving voice messages on both his cell phone and his direct office number. I did not receive a response.

We cannot want change for someone else more than they want it for themselves. To truly be successful, it was vital for him to be open to change, but it was clear to me that he was not committed to the essential adaptations that were desperately needed at that time.

Several months later, I found myself attending the same business event as this prospective client. When the opportunity presented itself, I asked him how things were going, and he shared with me that he was miserable. His bombastic, forceful, strong-willed style had continued to show up on a daily basis. His no-nonsense approach and his blunt, controlling, and unwilling-to-compromise manner were character flaws that needed to be wiped out sooner rather than later if he was going to be able to turn things around in his business. It was at this point that we seriously started our work together. It took time to register with him that he had used his desire to save money by initially not engaging my services as a way to convince himself that he didn't have any flaws. He was oblivious to how his self-absorbed, bullying tendencies had battered and bruised relationships across his organization and beyond. Eventually, he realized how dangerously close he had come to losing his company. His deep-rooted issues took a long time to unravel before we could rebuild the fabric of who he was. His dedication to recalibrate his thoughts and actions allowed him to gradually be able to interact in a respectful way with others by embodying a healthier leadership style. He instinctively knew that he wanted to make a difference, but he had been ignorant as to how he was showing up.

Understanding both the positive and negative perceptions of what others think of us is a healthy part of interpersonal growth. Gaining this type of perspective provides a more accurate interpretation of reality and an additional layer of self-awareness.

Top Nuggets of Wisdom

1 Perception is reality. The attitudes we project and the words we speak, along with the body language we exude, can be a game changer in a positive or negative way.

2 Whether we are running a marathon during extreme conditions or looking to expand our career, how we show up makes a difference in the outcomes of our lives.

3 We cannot want change for someone else more than they want it for themselves.

CHAPTER 11

Dial Up Your Brand

Whether we realize it or not, we each have an existing personal brand. Our personal brand is the impression we make merged with the reputation we create intentionally, or by default, in society. The majority of people have a brand that has been created by default. Our reputation could be one of respect and admiration, or it could be one that is significantly tarnished. Every one of us has been inflicted with libel or slander at some point in our lives. When we are falsely judged or purposely misrepresented, it takes a great deal of time and effort to re-establish our reputation. Sometimes, the damage is so severe that it can take years, and I am even aware of cases where it has been irreparable. Our brand image will vary from time to time and person to person based upon the experiences and perspectives of others in relation to us.

We have all judged others and others have judged us. Our beliefs, opinions, and assumptions about others aren't always based upon facts. Impression accuracy varies. Even well-intended individuals can have a bias in their views about someone or something. Our expectations frequently influence our visual perceptions. With the strong power of initial perceptions, it is a value add to be intentional about actively managing our brand. First impressions, good or bad, can be everlasting. It is not only our words that impact our brand:

body language influences it as well. Reputation management is about intentionally taking charge of and favorably influencing our image by authentic means. Our reputation can greatly influence how we are regarded as well as how we are treated. Every single one of our actions can build up, ding, or even ruin our reputation.

A few years ago, I volunteered to serve on a steering committee for an inaugural speakers' event. The call went out for speakers and the response was beyond what we could have hoped for. The final list of speakers went through an extensive vetting process until it was narrowed down to a group of five. All of the speakers were presumed to be of high integrity. The event went off flawlessly. About a week after the event, someone who I knew well and who had been in the audience that evening approached me. He divulged that one of the speakers had plagiarized his presentation. He went on to share that he had just watched a video that was almost identical to the speech that this participant had delivered. I sat with this information for a while before taking any action. Casting aspersions on someone else's character shouldn't be taken lightly, so I felt that it was best to raise the unsettling news with the chair of the committee. With forethought, the chair suggested that it would be best to just let it go. I felt as if I had been slapped across the face. My truthfulness had allowed me to believe that each of us who had been involved in this inaugural event felt the same way about his or her brand because each of us owned our own business. I was immobilized with the realization that the feelings that I had about how we preserve our brand were not reciprocal. In my world, the presenter was clearly wrong in passing off someone else's work as his own, but the chair was equally at fault when he blatantly shirked his responsibilities by not having a conversation with this presenter. It is one thing to spark an initial creative idea from viewing someone else's work, but it is another thing completely to copy someone else's body of work and pass it off as your own. I now have a less than favorable view of both the chair and the presenter.

When there is a valid experience of compromised character, even the most powerful endorsements become tainted.

Personal branding is the process of uncovering, communicating, and managing our image. It is a vital tool in building our career by differentiating ourself with regard to our strengths, skills, values, and passions. Our personal brand is created by how we show up in all aspects of our life. It includes our experiences, education, results, and verbal and nonverbal behaviors, combined with our physical appearance. It also takes into consideration who and what we surround ourself with – our entire package. The way we embody these traits can help us stand out from others to clearly convey our unique values. Over time, our personal brand becomes our reputation, as well as how people describe us to others, and how they relate to us.

Self-awareness extends an opportunity to expand courage and mental strength. Even successful leaders who reached the top made bad decisions along the way, but they had the humbleness to correct them. Our reputation is not defined by our mistakes: it is defined by the way we respond to them. People respect those who have the bravery to admit when they are wrong and then work to remedy their blunders. Humility is not a sign of weakness – it is a behavior that is admired. Possessing openness and self-reflection serves to expand our humility skills. Those who are transparent and share their missteps, especially when this includes lessons learned, gain credibility and trust.

Striving for personal excellence requires us to be the CEO of our own lives. We are solely responsible for shaping our personal brand, including boosting brand awareness and brand equity. Our day-to-day decisions, words, and actions all influence our reputation. Personal branding is impacted by what people think and say about us both behind closed doors and when we leave the room. It is best to manifest ourselves in the most genuine way possible. Strong brand recognition presents more opportunities and nurtures achievement.

I have found the most favorable traits for personal branding to be credibility, reliability, capability, humility, and trustworthiness. When we are able to take the time to examine what we do, why we do it, what we think, and why we think it, we can figure out the principles that drive us.

No two people are the same, even with identical twins. I know this firsthand because I have provided leadership coaching, mentoring, and advising to identical twins. Even though they have the same genome, their personalities, styles, approaches, experiences, views, and goals are just as distinct as they are with any two people. Successful personal branding is also about identifying the qualities that differentiate us. It is just as important to know who we are as it is to know who we are not. To be authentic, we need to have a clear understanding of our values, our purpose, and our vision.

Being the CEO of our own life also requires surrounding ourself with solid relationships. Investing in all-star people is worth its weight in gold. We all have blind spots, so it is imperative that we discover and then connect with people who we can trust and who can trust us in return. It is impossible to know everything about every topic, so being able to obtain sound advice from those who we value leads to smarter decision-making and better outcomes.

Just like companies have different divisions, so do we. Think about the categories in your life that are important to you and decide which ones are your highest priority. Here are some that are consequential to me and that you may also want to consider: health, fitness, psychological development, education, career, finances, social life, colleagues, home, family, friends, and spirituality. It is vital to assess where you are in each of your priority areas on a regular basis to make sure you are staying on track for your life strategy and your vision.

It is also important to understand what is of importance to your target audience. Everything that is visual sends a message that communicates who you are. This applies to how you present yourself during face-to-face encounters, messages you send via text, phone, or email, and the images you post online. Bear in mind that others can easily misinterpret your intentions or something that you say or do without you even realizing it.

Your personal value system is going to add to, or take away from, you reaching your vision. We all know someone who can turn the charisma on and off contingent upon the clout of the person with whom they are interacting. These individuals do not make respectable leaders. When someone has a situational value system, it is evidence of a person with bad character. I am particularly sensitive to and mindful of how others treat people in service-related industries. I have worked in retail, in restaurants, and in a wide variety of other service-related positions. On several occasions, I remember being treated poorly by those who thought that they were better than me. Someone's status or title shouldn't be the reason we bend over backwards for them. When a person displays discriminatory behaviors, their personal brand takes a hit.

Dialing up your brand puts an emphasis on actively managing the "benefit of you" both personally and professionally. Communication tends to be at the core of both our personal and our professional branding including visual, written, verbal, and nonverbal. There is much richness that can be obtained from nonverbal cues. Gestures as common as an expression on our face, or how we sit or stand, can share our state of mind. These primary forms of communication give insight into our personal brand. A blend of these communications contributes to how others view us and can impact our personal brand in a favorable or less than favorable way.

The art of thinking and the art of active listening are two far-reaching areas that are often underestimated with regard to how they add to or take away from our brand. Our world moves at such a frenzied pace that we inevitably find ourselves listening at a very low rate of comprehension. The best place to find a peaceful haven is in our own mind if we can dare to be quiet, to listen, and to seek understanding.

A solid brand image is essential for opening doors to career advancement. It is important to monitor your brand on a consistent basis. Your personal brand is distinctive to you – your unique promise of your true worth.

For an extended reach, it can be advantageous to leverage an individual's personal brand with their organization's brand, as long as one isn't adversely impacting the other. A credible personal or professional image is based on perceived trust.

A client of mine decided that they would reassess the financial advisory firm that they were using. They no longer wanted to work with a major brokerage house because they felt that they were "just a number." My client had searched for a firm whose belief system mirrored their own. My client knew that this would need to be a truly independent firm whose focus was to put the client first. They ended up selecting their new financial advisory firm specifically because of its solid reputation; it was founded on trust. Its company's culture embodied what resonated with my client. Its business model focused on developing long-term relationships. It accomplished this by providing clear and consistent communications and paying special attention to even the smallest of details. The firm has lived up to its brand by providing customized financial guidance that supports my client's wants, needs, expectations, and dreams.

Organizational branding is central for success. Just as an individual's brand represents a person's behaviors which are made up of beliefs, attitudes, experiences, assumptions, interests, and habits, a company's brand is very similar. Its brand consists of attitudes, behaviors, beliefs, and assumptions within a group. Your company's brand directly reflects your company's culture. When we think about corporate culture, each business needs to cultivate its atmosphere in a way that best supports its desired company brand. Those in a position of authority need to be more mindful of what their existing brand is conveying and then adjust it accordingly. To retain brand recognition, commerce needs to respond to countless outside factors on a daily basis irrespective of the industry, the size of the company, or the business's longevity. All businesses can add value in this area – even those with stellar brand recognition. Your company's DNA carries all of the information about your business, which is why it is imperative that it be at the heart of your company's brand strategy. Investing time and money into your brand is a smart business decision and can surprisingly be a game changer if managed properly.

Top Nuggets of Wisdom

1 Our brand is the impression we make merged with the reputation we create, intentionally or by default, in society.

2 Whether we realize it or not, we each have an existing personal brand. The majority of people and many companies have a brand that has been created by default.

3 Personal branding is the process of uncovering, communicating, and managing our image. It is a vital tool in building our career by differentiating ourself with regard to our strengths, skills, values, and passions.

CHAPTER 12

Curious

C uriosity has the power to kindle our lives with happiness. It amplifies our well-being and the overall essence of our world. Seizing the pleasures that go along with an inquiring mind can expand meaning in our lives. Nurturing our curiosity helps us to feel more alive and more engaged. It grants us more of an opportunity to embrace, connect with, and experience deeper moments of insight and meaning. Curiosity provides a strengthened infrastructure for a richer, more mindful, and overall fulfilling life. Be open and curious to stretch and seek out occasions to make a detour beyond your familiar routines.

Frequently, when I ask people what they truly want most, they will say that they want happiness. My clients have expressed that being happy is at a higher level of importance to them than their desire for knowledge, power, or wealth. Each of us has a different interpretation of what happiness looks like, and we are all entitled to our own individual viewpoints. Creativity is fueled by curiosity. Cultivating a curious mind can help us to unfold our life plans. When we harness the power of curiosity by capitalizing on our intelligence, wisdom, and relationships, happiness is often expanded.

A family business client hired me to help them unravel what would be their next step. The business was prospering under the leadership of the third generation; however, there was significant hostility between the family members that was centered on whether they should retain or sell the business. With most family businesses, there is an expectation, implied or otherwise, that each succeeding generation would work in the business. As this business had been passed down, the passion that the prior generations had felt had become diluted by the time it had reached the third generation. Our work together hammered away at identifying what each family member candidly wanted. For the first time in a long time, they felt the freedom that comes with remaining curious. This opportunity was a refreshing first for them. They became excited for what their future could bear. After much deliberation and internal turmoil, the current patriarch made the burdensome decision to sell the business. The family successfully sold the company and each family member then transitioned to a happier phase in life. Though they missed the stability and comfort of the family business, the sale allowed them to spread their wings. The family stressors of the past have now subsided. With my support, they put forth the extra effort towards mending the familial bond to create relationships that are stronger than ever. There are some family businesses that can go beyond the third generation successfully, but this particular one had reached its peak. There are few relationships in our lives that are meant to exist in perpetuity, but not everyone has the honesty and the courage to know when things have reached their high-water mark. I applaud these clients for their inquisitiveness to venture into the unknown for a better quality of life.

Curiosity expands intellect, wonder, and intrigue. Increasing our satisfaction and meaning in life comes when we remain curious and center our time and energy on special interests or pursuits. A well-balanced, inquisitive learner generates enthusiasm, energy, and confidence, and often expands their range of interests. Nurturing an attitude of openness and genuine interest sparks healthier relationships.

The greater the depth and breadth of our curiosity, the better the options we have to encounter things that excite and inspire us to expand to our next level of success.

I was cleaning out one of my file cabinets. During that process, I stumbled upon a folder that had an old letter from a dear childhood friend who had initially started off as my summer camp counselor. She now lives many states away and we haven't seen each other in more years than I can remember. I had completely forgotten about this priceless sentiment. This literary trip down memory lane was amazingly nostalgic with reminiscences of all of the great times that we had shared.

She wrote,

> *Most of all, I remember the special friendship we developed. What stood out about you most was your confidence and your determination. You may not have felt or understood that about yourself back then, but I always admired that about you. You knew what you wanted, and you were not afraid to go for it. You were smart and had an inner beauty that I knew would be your driving force as you made your life decisions. It looks like it has served you well.*

As I re-read this, I had no idea that was how she felt or that I had showed up in the way that she had described. Ironically, how she experienced me back then was so completely opposite of how I was actually feeling at that time. I had no idea who I was; I was completely lacking in self-confidence. Like most other kids, I was nothing more than a confused, insecure young person who was trying to figure out the overwhelming complexities of life.

We don't often think about what is remarkable about our own selves. We are all unique in our styles, approaches, and life experiences. Understanding the qualities that others admire most about us is powerful. We can gain strength from that awareness and leverage it to make sound choices, giving our minds the space to find better paths forward.

We each process what we hear and what we see in our own unique way. As a result, it is wise to operate from a place of greater understanding and genuine compassion. When we sincerely foster more curiosity, and minimize the inclination to be judgmental, we open ourselves up to unlimited possibilities. How stimulating it feels to be able to feed and balance our minds with an assortment of beliefs and opinions. How invigorating it is to be open to exchanging ideas that may broaden our knowledge and even upgrade our perspectives. How electrifying it is to be able to clarify, to sharpen, and then to strengthen our current viewpoint.

It is not possible for one person to know everything, and yet it seems to be especially difficult at the executive level to ask for support. It is not a sign of weakness for an executive to admit to the need for help: it is a sign of wisdom and enhanced leadership.

People who seek advice and help from others are looked upon more favorably and have better outcomes than those who never reach out because they believe that they have all of the answers. Reaching out for input and insights from others does not make us appear incompetent – it is just the opposite. When we put our egos and our vulnerabilities aside, our curiosity will allow us to enhance ourselves by truly learning from others. This kind of intellectual development pays dividends throughout our life. Experiences from the past can enhance our future if we remain open-minded and intellectually curious.

When we choose to remain curious, we are actually able to think more deeply about things. It allows us to self-examine. Remaining curious gives us permission to rethink, reorganize, and reinvent ourselves for a renewed sense of self-direction. The power of intellectual curiosity supports our thoughts, which affects our inner being, our attitudes, and our happiness. Striving for more balance will create a better quality of life. If you are able to listen to your body, your mind, and your heart, you will learn to recognize when you can just listen to others, and when it is time to lean in and capitalize by sharing your own wisdom and experiences. It is also essential to know when things have unexpectedly escalated should you need to withdraw to take care of yourself.

When I reflect over my client base, the common thread is that they are all inquisitive. Dedicated lifelong learners are curious at their core. Their natural interest in learning helps them to stay engaged so that they have a profound impact in all aspects of their lives. Throughout the course of their lives, those who are able to remain curious can and do tap into their retained knowledge as needed.

Curious people are often open-minded to the insights and opinions of others. They are generally supportive, collaborative, and innovative and they are usually non-blaming and non-shaming. Curious people ask who, what, when, where, and why. They adapt to change by understanding the positive and negative effects of the past with an innovative focus that is geared towards ways to improve and make the future better. No one has all of the answers; however, curious people are more likely to unearth problems and then resolve them for the betterment of our world.

Our unique styles are influenced by a blend of factors such as experiences, education, and maturity. We become more effective when we understand our own style and are able to assess the styles of those around us. People can relate better when we understand each other's preferences and priorities. When we take the time to comprehend what motivates others and how their motivations may differ from our own, we are able to build more effective relationships.

The next time you find yourself having a disagreement with someone, think about how your priorities, stressors, and past experiences might be shaping each of your viewpoints. Use that as a golden nugget to change the conversation to one that reaps collaboration, enthusiasm, and support.

Successful innovators have a natural appetite for learning. By being proactive, present, and aware, we can learn and grow in support of the space between where we are today and where we want to be in the future. Challenges are often an opportunity for us to learn more about ourselves and those who we surround ourselves with. We often acquire the most knowledge during the most difficult times in our lives: the times when things feel that they have moved beyond what we can handle. Remaining curious allows us to continue to make traction even during those highly demanding periods in our lives.

It is important to think about what it is that you really want. Once you know that, you can define what happiness looks like for you and then go out and make it happen. By putting one foot in front of the other, you will be able to make one decision at a time, one action at a time. Be assured that if you are learning, you are progressing.

Those who are naturally curious have an innate openness to learn and to improve. They are able to pinpoint the joy in their world, allowing them to add meaning to their own life as well as to the lives of those who they surround themselves with. These creative minds accept change because they are receptive to fresh ideas and new possibilities. It is a beneficial habit to be able to appreciate and enjoy where you are today while concurrently looking for ways to continue to evolve. Enjoy the adventure as you learn from your past, embrace today, and blueprint your tomorrow.

Top Nuggets of Wisdom

1 Curiosity has the power to kindle our lives with happiness. It amplifies our well-being and the overall essence of our world.

2 Being happy is at a higher level of importance than the desire for knowledge, power, or wealth.

3 Increasing our satisfaction and meaning in life comes when we remain curious and center our time and energy on special interests or pursuits.

CHAPTER 13

Culture

Culture drives human dynamics. Culture is a collection of shared ideas, preferences, values, goals, and assumptions which represent the habits, manners, lifestyles, and pursuits as it relates to a specific group of individuals. The character and personality of any organization is its "culture." Culture can have a powerful impact in a positive and/or negative way.

We thrive when we feel connected and valued as part of the "heartbeat" of the group. People want to be in an environment where they can take pride in their work; they want to contribute and make a difference in a meaningful way. Involved individuals enjoy working where there is a culture of growth, trust, respect, purpose, flexibility, and effective communication.

Being energized by seeing the impact that we make is a compelling motivator to refresh and renew our commitment to productivity. There is greater enthusiasm and a stronger connection when we have a sense of purpose. We tend to contribute more when there is a personal connection – when we know how our specific work makes a difference to the bottom line.

Our distinctions in aptitude, experience, education, ideas, and points of view all help to develop a broader "think-tank": a groundswell of excellence. A robust culture elevates retention and increases the probability of higher-quality referral hires. It supports the development of healthy employees both physically and emotionally, which reduces absenteeism and tardiness. Additionally, it accelerates capacity, profitability, and organic growth. High-spirited employees tend to be more attuned to the needs of the business and its customers. They are more observant in terms of processes, standards, and systems, all of which provide for a greater commitment to quality and safety. Inspiring others to be their best selves can be a game changer. A healthy culture fuels all aspects of the business including more purposeful employees, happier customers, increased brand recognition, and greater financial results.

Our world is changing minute-by-minute, exposing us to an ever-changing array of unimaginable new risks. Without steadfast attention, irreversible results may occur. The relentless acceleration of demands is unsustainable. People are a finite resource. If we are confronted with one challenging decision after another, not only will the quality of our choices drastically diminish – we will also likely feel demoralized. Those who are known to "get it done" without any fanfare ironically find themselves on the short end of the stick with more and more work assigned to them. We are now witnessing even workaholics and overachievers with depleted mental tanks. Placing a focus on a culture that embodies a caring attitude has never been needed more.

Our workforce, especially millennials, desire to work for companies that will help them to be able to thrive. Employee engagement accrues when steady progress is generated in a meaningful and flexible way. Various research polls tout that much of our workforce is unengaged. The upshot is that the majority of employees are resentful and even act out because they feel that their needs are not being met. Without executives even realizing it, these unengaged workers can kill profits with staggering hidden costs. It is important to understand the true outlay associated with disconnected personnel. They include, but are not limited to, bringing down morale, reduced retention of employees, higher absenteeism, abuse of sick time, consistent tardiness, increases in mistakes, minimal job growth, and lower productivity. For publicly traded companies there is a reduction in share price. When people feel stagnant and bored they get into a habit of just going through the motions because they don't care. A spirit of "I couldn't care less!" results in mistakes and accidents taking place more frequently, which eventually drives away customers. When people feel that they are not important and that their efforts aren't appreciated, a downward spiral is launched that puts profitability on the chopping block.

Estimates indicate that unengaged employees cost the United States alone hundreds of billions of dollars every year – a massive number. Lack of engagement can usually be linked to incompetent leadership. When your employees, who are also your brand's ambassadors, are not happy, it is poison for your company's reputation and credibility. It is vitally important to never underestimate the power of employee engagement within your business. Everyone within the ecosystem of a business should be taken into consideration and treated with kindness and respect. Each of us has a unique set of strengths that provides value. Different doesn't mean better or worse: it is just different. The most successful organizations remain nimble and capitalize on the unique merits that each person brings.

The CEO of a human resources technology company was referred to me by one of my long-term clients. This technology company was having a revolving door issue with employee retention. Unfortunately, its leadership did not appreciate the importance of building into the fabric of the business the range of multiple generational needs which was paramount if it was to become a sustainable, competitive, agile, and linked organization. This intergenerational disconnect escalated into a crisis, which was when I was invited to come on the scene. There were clearly different values, different expectations, and different life experiences across all levels of the organization. This meant that there was a need for new skills to be developed and new employment practices to be implemented to bring a wider view of the company's diverse cultural dynamics and work behaviors. The ongoing demands on the entire staff required establishing highly interactive and agile teams that were made up of supercharged individuals with unique skills and abilities. We worked on reshaping teams, organizational units, and processes to create "dream teams." It was imperative that employees were able to connect and communicate across all levels of the company if they were to respond effectively to constantly changing needs. This strategy was also extended to how departments were reorganized, and to how employees were assessed and compensated. Getting employees to initially interact, and ultimately to collaborate, increased employee engagement so that value-added knowledge flowed freely across multiple generations. This effort expanded employee relations and transitioned the learning environment at all levels.

Organizational transformation does not happen overnight. In this situation, there were a number of "naysayers" who eventually became believers once the generational transition strategy became a model for success. This company is now more focused on the variations that people bring to the table because leadership witnessed firsthand how differences can serve to be an advantage.

We should be checking the satisfaction of our staff on a regular basis. Employee engagement surveys are helpful and are often used to gain a deeper understanding of the human energy within a business. The results will often vary by individuals, teams, and divisions. It is just as important to look at the overarching results as it is to understand feedback at a more granular level. When employee engagement surveys are done well, they can be very valuable as early warning signs. They can also provide a great deal of insight into what is really going on in the company so that swift action can be taken in the specific areas that need improvement. Many companies purely guess at what they think is wrong and then make changes based upon their incorrect hypotheses. The consequence of this is that the true issues do not get resolved.

Through various employee engagement survey results that my colleagues and I have been privy to, we have seen that a consistent strain in manager–employee relationships has emerged. Employees often leave because of their direct manager/supervisor. I believe this is the primary reason the workforce has such low engagement. I have seen this chronic problem remedied when all levels of leadership are properly trained and focused on fostering engaged, productive relationships with their teams. The most effective managers make it their highest priority to connect the work their team is doing with the ultimate goals the company is working towards.

The most successful leaders shape organizational culture by their own attitudes and actions. They understand that company culture needs to be at the core of their business model. Organizations with engaged, happier personnel outperform their competition; it is a competitive advantage.

Generational differences at work are one of the top challenges that my clients struggle with. Having five generations in the labor force presents a new diversity challenge that most leaders are unprepared for. Workforce behaviors vary between the traditionalists, baby boomers, Generation X, Generation Y, and Generation Z. Many seasoned leaders miss out on new and exciting opportunities because they believe that the sole focus should be on providing mentoring opportunities for the younger generations to be partnered with those who are more experienced; they don't see that the younger generations have value to provide to the more seasoned professionals as well. When we are open to appreciating the value of a diverse labor force, we can best capitalize on the styles and approaches of each. The most successful outcomes are brought about through the combined cultural familiarity and currency of skills, experiences, mindsets, and knowledge that each generation, and everyone within it, brings to the greater good.

A multibillion-dollar publicly traded company asked me to advise their senior leadership team on how best to navigate the differences in the various generations within their workforce. Their leaders were unwavering in their desire to rid the company of what had become a toxic culture. The feedback that they had received through their employee engagement survey was that some of the younger managers were feeling insecure. They felt that they lacked the knowledge to supervise older employees who had more work experience than they had, but who were their direct reports. Older managers also admitted to an underlying strain and a disconnect because of this culture gap. The generational tension was ravaging this company's progress. The best action forward was to gain awareness and buy-in across all levels of this business with the goal being to accelerate away from the generational stereotypes. Moving beyond the judgmental labeling was the only way this organization was going to rise above this systemic issue. We created a program where freshly minted college graduates were paired with baby boomers, since those two groups represented the biggest opportunity for improvement. With the right scripting, consistent messaging, and the commitment of everyone involved to remain open-minded, this reciprocal style of mentoring paid off with dividends. They learned to pay less attention to their differences and to focus instead on the unique values that each employee brought to the table. This turned out to be the optimal way to expunge their toxic environment. Once they were able to reduce the competitive and subjective views that they each held, camaraderie was able to flow, which then resulted in the acquisition of the necessary traction towards an overall improved culture. This was most noticeable in the areas of employee retention and the design and implementation of critical projects. Their senior leadership team was committed to concentrating on both the short- as well as the long-term results for the betterment of the organization as a whole. The team's harmonic actions inspired and incentivized employees to work collaboratively together. This company continues to maintain a pulse through periodic employee surveys. The honest, anonymous responses that are culled from these questionnaires allow it to regularly adapt to its shifting demographics and the changing needs of its employees. It can now sustain its healthy culture.

There can be huge implications for employers in how they manage the needs and expectations of the various age cohorts within any company. Tapping into the multiple talents of all employees empowers personal and organizational achievement. The most successful companies disregard ageism completely and capitalize instead on the distinct sets of skills, beliefs, and values that each person can provide.

Building a strong company culture fosters feelings of group character which support our common-thread need for solidarity. A stimulating culture is a big piece of the overall equation when it comes to success and fulfillment. Those leaders who invest in cultivating their keystone assets have a significant advantage. It is extremely important that people feel connected to the impact of their work and are aware that they are creating important business results. When employers take care of their employees' essential needs, it becomes second nature for employees to then take care of their employer's business needs. Enhanced engagement with all associates is the primary ingredient to sustainable success in all aspects of commerce.

To construct a solid culture, find out what motivates your employees: learn what is important to them. Often leaders assume that they know what makes their employees feel engaged and happy based on their own views of what makes them happy, and often they are wrong. To create a hallmark team, open the lines of communication by including your team in the decision-making process. Organizations experience greater success with engagement and improve business performance when they treat employees as stakeholders of their own future as well as of the company's future. Senior leaders who put energy into making sure that their employees are engaged set their organization apart from their competition. There is no "correct" company culture – every business is different. Take the time to identify and highlight what makes your company unique, and then decide how to regularly convey the new and improved culture. Remember to model the desired behaviors both in everyday practices and from a strategic long-term planning perspective.

There is a well-known saying that rings true about how individuals may forget what you say or do, but they don't forget how you made them feel. Empathy is a skill that is critical in our modern society. When we authentically focus on helping others to feel valued, respected, and appreciated, we are letting them know that they are important. Each interaction and experience we have sparks a culmination of feelings and emotions. As a leader, you will be remembered by the impact of your understanding, your compassion, and your kindness, rather than a random list of accomplishments. To best support group harmony, agile leaders know how to listen and then how to best respond.

Organizations need to live and breathe in a culture that is flourishing. Highly engaged employees are the primary driver for real business growth and achievement. We need to be more aware of creating and maintaining a culture that truly appreciates the value of our workforce. Leaders can assess the engagement of their employees by taking a quick pulse:

1. Are employees physically present at work but seemingly either preoccupied or inattentive?
2. Are employees tardy on an ongoing basis?
3. Has employee absenteeism increased?
4. Do employees attend and contribute during meetings?
5. Do employees lack productivity?
6. Do employees partake equally in collaborative efforts?
7. Do employees exhibit attention to detail?
8. Do employees complete work on time and within budget?
9. Is there a trend where there is a slip in quality?

If the answer is "Yes" to even one of these "red flag" questions above, it is time for a serious call to action: the organization is not in good health. Even though we traditionally assess a company by its bottom line, engaged versus unengaged employees is really the best indicator of an organization's long-term viability.

Many muddled situations occur with the belief that compensation can bring happiness. Money is necessary for survival, but money alone cannot buy happiness, vigor, or trusting relationships. More money will certainly bring comfort and an enhanced lifestyle, but there is no guarantee that it will bring fulfillment, which is at the core of highly committed employees. We all regard money differently; everyone's relationship to money is idiosyncratic. When we fixate on compensation, it can dilute the possibilities of finding genuine satisfaction. How much compensation is enough for each one of us is very individual.

When people are too focused on the financial aspect of things, it can prevent them from enjoying not just their job, but their life. I have worked with clients who hated their job, but they were so accustomed to the lifestyle that their income provided that they felt trapped. To them, there were no alternatives but to stay miserable in their work just to maintain the lifestyle that they and their family had become accustomed to.

Monetary benefits used to be the main motivator and driving force for productive outcomes. Today, it is a blend of many things, not just financial incentives. Human beings are motivated by a mixture of different things. I have found that we perform best when we are intellectually stimulated, feel valued, and receive appropriate compensation for the position that we hold. Dovetailing employee interests and skills with relevant tasks, while also providing an equitable wage, can lead to optimal performance. Motivating a workforce requires individualization and customization – there is no "one size fits all" approach.

Leadership is so much more than just attaining financial objectives. Leaders need to set the tone to future-proof their organizations, and in so doing they will also advance their own careers. Leadership is about doing the right thing even if no one else knows about it – even when it is terrifying and uncomfortable. A company's culture can shine, or it can hide behind ethical misconduct. Illegal or unethical behavior at work can have serious consequences if unaddressed. Speaking up about a serious issue in the workplace may be viewed as disloyal because it can easily turn into an explosive minefield. Turning a blind eye is not high principled, but it allows us to remain uninvolved. We all have choices when it comes to whether or not we compromise our ethical values. Smart leaders stay true to their code of ethics by mobilizing their moral courage and leading by example.

A high-potential leader in corporate America that I was working with was asked to enhance a special "pet" project that had huge revenue potential. He was excited to be given the opportunity to lead the expansion of this "sleeping giant." Unfortunately, while doing his due diligence, he uncovered a fatal flaw in the process: a significant legality issue was revealed that required that either meaningful changes be made quickly to the program, or it be shut down completely. Ceasing operations would mean the loss of this revenue stream. Based on his research, this violation could cause the board of directors to go to jail. As his coach, I had numerous conversations with him about how best to move this intense situation forward. Once he had completely digested the gravity of this compliance issue, his integrity would not allow him to keep these details to himself.

As the exceptional leader that he was, he felt that it was his responsibility to not only make sure that the appropriate people were aware of the violation, but to also provide a legitimate solution to keep the program going. Significant changes would need to be made to transition the program into compliance, but it could be done if the desire was there. He presented his findings to the corporate attorney who was responsible for this program. The attorney was shocked to hear what my client's research had uncovered. The attorney told my client that he was uninformed about his allegations, but that he was deeply concerned. My client presented him with three choices: the attorney could bring up the issue with the executive in charge of this program himself, they could collaboratively raise the issue together, or my client would undertake things on his own. The in-house attorney decided that my client should be the one to not only present his findings, but to also relate the extensive plans to resolve the issue that my client had laboriously created.

The work that my client and I had done together had taught him that if he needed to challenge someone or something, he needed to have at least one potential solution to bring forth. He requested a meeting with the senior vice president of sales to share his findings. This executive was well known for "blowing a gasket" when things weren't going his way. The news that my client had to share was less than favorable, which meant that he was going to be on the "hot seat" and that a full interrogation would ensue.

Opening Pandora's box is nothing short of intense. To be fully prepared, I encouraged him to double- and triple-check all of his research as well as the presentation itself. I also advised him to check in with himself right before he walked into the meeting to make sure that he was composed emotionally. As anticipated, the senior vice president erupted like a volcano. My client told me later that he had embedded in his thoughts to never treat anyone the way he was treated at that moment – such condescension and disrespect – especially when my client was trying to do what was best not just for the company, but also for the senior vice president's career. After all, this catastrophe occurred on his watch. The senior vice president chastised my client: "Who do you think you are?" His tongue-lashing continued with the reminder that my client wasn't an attorney, and that the company had an entire legal team who were responsible for finding any improprieties that might exist. My client explained that he was not trying to be an attorney, nor was he trying to step on anyone else's toes. His actions were based on living and breathing the code of values that the company had established, and because of that he felt that it was important to bring forward the problem and offer some possible solutions. My client shared that he had stumbled upon his findings purely by accident and queried, "Do you really think I would come to you with such a serious situation if I wasn't 100% sure? Doing that would be self-sabotage and career-altering." He added that he had already spoken with the attorney who was responsible for this program, and even he was unaware of the infringements that my client had uncovered. The senior vice president's response was that he had a hard time believing my client's findings.

The next morning, my client's attendance was requested at a meeting with the general counsel and a few key executives. On some level, my client was grateful that things were coming to a head because he had been losing sleep over the matter ever since the initial discovery. Though he wasn't second-guessing his decision to bring this crucial information forward, he was perplexed as to why he was the one being verbally abused. He was feeling very uncomfortable. Not only had he found the problem, but he was trying to bring awareness to the proper internal authorities while also trying to fix the compliance issue. I gave my client a pep talk. Even though what he was doing was extremely stressful, he was doing the right thing. I knew that he had been raised with strong values. Though he was scared and intimidated by what was taking place, I believed that he could muster the courage and the strength to see this through to the best of his abilities, even if it meant losing his job. He was bound and determined to not compromise his values and beliefs.

He sat across from the general counsel and shared specifics about all that he had unmasked. When he was done, the general counsel put his face between the palms of his hands, shook his head back and forth and said, "He is right. We need to shut this program down ASAP," – and they did just that. The attorney who was responsible for this program lost his job shortly thereafter.

Once we "peel back the onion" and find errors, intentional or not, they need to be escalated to the level within the organization where the proper decisions can be made to correct these flaws.

Moral consciousness needs to be amplified during all management decisions: from the company vision, to the mission, to the code of conduct, to the work environment, to expectations, and even to goals. The most important wisdom is learned and earned through experience. We profit not only from our own mistakes, but also from observing and improving our minds through the mistakes of others. Those who rely upon our leadership take cues from us. C-suite executives need to be on the frontlines of their company culture. This influential position creates healthier human intellectual achievement to master conditions of advanced growth. When the going gets rough, leaders need to focus and leverage their guiding principles by finessing their vision to inspire others to excel.

It is easy for heads of companies to overlook culture. Often, they consider "feelings" to be too "fluffy." One of my long-standing clients and I often talked about his skeptical views of what he perceives to be a "touchy-feely" skill. He struggles to see the business worth. His direct, competitive, decisive, risk-taking personality has difficulty relating to "feelings" in the workplace. I asked him if he'd entertain the idea of doing an interesting interpersonal test before our next session. As I described the exercise, his body language told me that this was going to be very difficult for him. He felt strongly that it was not going to make any difference, and that it was a waste of his time in a schedule that was already overflowing with demands. He hesitantly agreed to the trial after saying that I had always provided sound guidance and that he trusted me. I explained that his employees wanted to feel connected to him, and for that to happen he needed to soften his approach to meet them where they were. I went on to explain that he needed to think positively about this exercise, and to also be extra observant with his employees for two weeks. The goal was "to catch" as many people as possible doing a good job and then to express genuine appreciation for their work efforts. He said that he felt uncomfortable doing that because "that is what I pay them to do." I asked him to remain curious and open-minded to see what happened if he showed up differently around the office. At our next session, he was holding back a grin on his face and finally confessed by saying,

> *WOW – the results were very different than I expected. After I got over how silly I felt giving someone a compliment for the work they were hired to do, I focused on the task at hand. As soon as I witnessed something being done well, I immediately responded with a compliment or an acknowledgment. People lit up! Some had a shocked look on their faces because they had no idea that I was watching. It sparked additional dialog with people that I've never really talked to before. There ended up being a ripple effect as many of the people I complimented told their co-workers and it became part of the 'water-cooler conversation' in a positive way.*

He went on to share that everyone seemed to have more pep in their step just by his taking notice of them. Convincing him to remain curious about making small changes in his organization's culture produced rewards on two levels: he gained valuable insights that he hadn't had before, and this tiny change that he finally had been willing to implement increased productivity, which then expanded his business.

Culture change is gradual. It takes time and it takes practice. Setbacks are natural and to be expected. Some days we move the lever forward and some days we don't. Every day is a new opportunity to go after what we truly want. Sometimes we may feel extremely overwhelmed to the point of feeling powerless for what to do next. Insecurity of this sort drives distorted thinking. To adjust your mindset from powerless to powerful, you must first acknowledge that just because you feel dead-ended does not mean you really are. We often underestimate how powerful we actually are. Approach challenges with an understanding that every problem has a solution. Even if you can't figure out the answer right away, have faith that every problem can be dealt with, solved, or overcome. Center your energy on taking control of what is within your control.

Top Nuggets of Wisdom

1 Culture drives human dynamics. Culture is a collection of shared ideas, preferences, values, goals, and assumptions which represent the habits, manners, lifestyles, and pursuits of a specific group of individuals.

2 We thrive when we feel connected and valued as part of the "heartbeat" of the group. People want to be in an environment where they can take pride in their work; they want to contribute and make a difference in a meaningful way.

3 Involved individuals enjoy working where there is a culture of growth, trust, respect, purpose, flexibility, and effective communication.

CHAPTER 14

Giving

Givers know the true power and benefits of altruistic behaviors. Givers give up their seat to a stranger on a bus or a train. They hold the elevator door so that someone else can fit in. They let someone who is behind them in line move up because they have fewer items. These simple acts of humanity could make someone's day. I try to reach out to others by phone, a quick text, or even the old-fashioned way of sending a card. I have had a number of people respond to my message saying that I had perfect timing because it had helped them to get over the hurdle that they were dealing with at that moment. When others remember us, it makes us feel special. These random acts of kindness can make a huge difference in someone else's life. It is a sad comment on our society to observe that many people rarely think about doing even the smallest courtesy for someone else because they are too caught up in their own "stuff." True philanthropy starts with generosity.

Many years ago, my dad was suffering from gallstones which required him to be admitted to the local hospital. Something as straightforward as gallstones quickly turned into a nightmare that required my dad to be hospitalized for 50 days. The gallstones had created a blockage that obstructed his pancreas. This intense situation eventually turned into pancreatitis. After removing the gallstones, the surgeons discovered two pseudocysts on his pancreas, both of which were the size of tangerines. The situation looked quite grave. The initial medical interventions didn't work, and he continued to spike a high fever. In addition, the medications he had been taking didn't work as they had been designed to. Even though the physicians used tube feeding that was going directly into his gastrointestinal tract, he wasn't able to retain enough calories, resulting in his weight dropping to a critical level. The physicians then tried a more aggressive food line called a TPN that pumped food directly into his bloodstream, but his health continued to fail. The usual treatments and protocols weren't working. The decision was made to perform emergency surgery to remove his gallbladder as a stopgap measure. What was unfolding was hard for us as a family to comprehend. My dad had never been sickly, so this state of affairs was frightening and left me feeling helpless. I wanted and needed to do something to help. I decided to donate blood on his behalf. After donating the initial time, I felt good about my contribution and made a promise to myself that I would donate again. Eight weeks later, when I went for my second blood donation, I learned that I possessed a rare blood type, Rh A negative. Realizing that I was in a special position to help others in crisis, I began donating blood on a regular basis. To date, I have donated over ten gallons of blood to those who are desperately in need.

Those of us who give more than we receive live the most fulfilling lives. However, it is important to be careful that we don't overextend ourselves. Those who are truly kind and generous to others are less apt to be taken advantage of because we remain conscientious about keeping our own goals in mind. A fresh dose of awareness for what we do for others, who we do it for, and when, where, and how – coupled with an emphasis on our own interests – allows us to flourish. We learn that we can do for others while simultaneously doing for ourselves.

I have collaborated with a professional connector whose passion for giving drives her to want to connect like-minded professionals where there might be some synergy. She does this daily without any reward or remuneration, and yet everyone values her as a colleague, a friend, a mentor, a business associate, and a deal maker. She has impeccable character, she is humble, she is well read, and she has accomplished this all without a college degree. Her brand has consistently been reinforced through social media. She is a sought-after guest speaker, instructor, and author. She does amazing work with businesses around the globe. If you ask her what her brand is she casually responds, "I just do what I do."

Most givers do not appreciate what they bring to the table because their focus is always on doing for others. The downside to this conduct is that givers often miss the mark because they put themselves last. Givers are so passionate about helping others that they frequently have nothing left for themselves. Healthy relationships should support the door swinging in both directions.

I need to confess that I have more times than not fallen into a pattern of selfless giving. At my core, I become energized helping others get to a better place with whatever their challenges are. The conundrum was that I was putting in significant hours to "do for others," but I was not scheduling the amount of time that was necessary to get my own work accomplished in every aspect of my life. I was not taking good care of me. I took a long, hard look in the mirror, and the woman who stared back at me was overweight, out of shape, stressed, sleep-deprived, largely unappreciated, and resentful. What I did not realize was that I had lost myself in my efforts to be selfless.

At that moment, I made a commitment to myself to start to change how I was living my life. I needed to learn to "put the oxygen mask on me first" if I was going to be better equipped to support others going forward. Self-care is not self-indulgence: it is self-preservation. It is still a constant battle for me. I often find myself burning the midnight oil and waking up before dawn to satisfy my overachieving expectations. When I am in the vicious cycle of exhaustion, I am not showing up as my best self. To improve in this area, I decided to adopt a new approach that I had heard about from one of my colleagues. The technique is "strategic giving." It instructs that we strive for a gentle balance of helping others to achieve their goals while respecting our own aspirations. I have become more aware of my Achilles heel in this area, and I am now able to redirect and take intentional steps to get myself back on track. I now schedule quiet time and productive "me" time. I find when I honor these dedicated spaces in my regular calendar, I have higher-quality outcomes, more productivity, and a healthier sense of well-being. Creating and maintaining these boundaries allows for a happier me, which allows for higher-quality exchanges with others. I am aware that I have turned a page and find that I am no longer resentful. We can only care for others if we don't lose ourselves in the process.

I often meet with clients who tell me that they do not have anyone who they truly trust in their life. They feel vulnerable because they are surrounded by "takers" who want something from them because of either their job title, their connections, or their wealth. These "takers" try to manipulate my clients for money, a job, an introduction, free tickets, a product, or a specialized service. My clients relate: "They don't care about me. It's all about what I can do for them." It is unfortunate, but there seem to be more and more of these opportunists whose primary angle is to look out for themselves. These people cannot create strong long-term alliances. They are toxic, and they burn through relationships by making others feel used and abused. Arrogance, ignorance, and greed are eating into the nucleus of human nature.

Some people are very giving in their personal life, and yet they show up differently in the work arena. They fear being taken advantage of if they are perceived as being too generous or too giving. I've often mused that it would be an interesting concept if performance reviews took into consideration an improved sense of merit for those who do more for others. Supporting a giving culture at our places of work would certainly make for a happier work lifestyle. Leaders who are able to strike the balance between adding significance to others while making sure to be productive themselves support higher outcomes for all employees, rather than just for themselves.

No one makes it alone – we all need a beacon of hope and help. A little assistance goes a long way, and the smallest act of kindness can change a life. If you don't already, I would encourage you to contribute to a world of generosity rather than a world of finagling. Givers have a desire to touch the lives of others in meaningful ways. They build their networks every day through their kind-hearted gestures. For them, teaching others how to succeed is a gratifying way of life. If we are altruistically generous, we will be able to provide credit where credit is due, and stronger collaborations will be the byproduct.

As leaders, a pay-it-forward opportunity to grow takes place when we put forth dedicated time and energy to support others. When we have the spirit from within to step forward and lend a helping hand, it kindles happiness and pays dividends for all involved. Giving of ourselves is the simplest way we can improve our well-being. There are many benefits that come from giving back, including an expanded sense of purpose, increased mental stimulation, and the opportunity to develop new skills by building upon our existing knowledge and experiences. Additionally, we have the good fortune to interface with new people who we might not cross paths with in our day-to-day personal and professional lives. If you aren't already doing so, consider offering your services as a volunteer as a way to help others.

One of my clients was sharing with me her views on volunteering. She said,

> *There is no amount of money in the world that can compare with the good feelings that I have experienced over the last eighteen*

years from serving on various non-profit boards in the community. I don't think that people truly get the message about how good giving back feels – or maybe it's just a message that many find irrelevant these days.

Promoting a better quality of life by making a difference in the civic life of our communities allows us to feel more connected. When we are feeling more connected, our leadership abilities expand, and we are more able to create positive social change. Giving back supports our sense of responsibility to our community and to the greater good. Being committed to the success of others by giving time, knowledge, and energy not only opens doors, but also helps to build solid connections. When we are shoulder to shoulder with others who are volunteering alongside us, a different kind of credibility gets established. Helping others sustains us as we explore who we are and how we fit into the world around us.

Top Nuggets of Wisdom

1 Givers know the true power and benefits of altruistic behaviors.

2 A fresh dose of awareness for what we do for others, who we do it for, and when, where, and how – coupled with an emphasis on our own interests – allows us to flourish.

3 Those who are truly kind and generous to others are less apt to be taken advantage of because we remain conscientious about keeping our own goals in mind. We learn that we can do for others while simultaneously doing for ourselves.

CHAPTER 15

Gratitude

Gratitude opens our eyes to a more optimistic view of the world. It is a favorable human emotion. Having "an attitude of gratitude" is a strength in character. Gratitude is more than just saying thank you. It is an appreciation that is expressed towards the goodness in our lives. Gratitude is magnified when it is an unexpected, selfless act of kindness. The power of sharing goodwill has immediate and long-lasting impact, creating a larger social circle of prosperity.

Thoughtful actions towards others play an active role in our physical and psychological well-being. Those of us who have an appreciative mindset are traditionally happier and have a greater degree of moral values. Acts of gratitude provide personal benefit and motivation for the giver as well as for the receiver. Gratitude helps us to treasure what we have received. Expressing appreciation benefits us because we feel good about returning the courtesy to those who have supported us. Those who receive the recognition have an equally inspiring effect. Generosity empowers an upward spiral of robust social relations. Interpersonal relationships are strengthened when gratitude is present; it fosters cohesiveness.

In our materialistic society, we have a tendency to aim our attention towards what we lack, or on what others have that we don't. When we become too familiar with our surroundings, the novelty can disappear, we start to take things for granted, and eventually our world seems boring. We see this played out when we have been driving the same car, living in the same house, having the same job, or being in the same intimate relationship. Human nature prompts us to believe that the grass is always greener on the other side. It is difficult to distinguish between what is sizzle and what is substance. We are attracted to novel sights, sounds, material objects, and experiences because they are new and stimulating. While some new things have the potential to expand our knowledge and experiences, they can also expose and teach us life lessons from the dark side.

The thrill of an acquisition is often short-lived. Possessions are often less gratifying than the simple pleasures of spending time with those who we feel closely connected to. Oftentimes, we do not realize the true value of a person or things of consequence until something goes amiss. When we fail to appreciate and acknowledge the importance of people, places, and specific things in our life, those complacent assumptions can breed inconsiderate behaviors, which in turn compromises the stability and confidence in the status quo of our lives.

The essence of sharing knowledge, insight, and wisdom has a lasting impact in the greater scheme of things. During my college years, I worked as a purchasing agent at a technology start-up that had about 70 employees. One day, for no special reason that I was aware of, my manager asked to speak with me in his office. He seemed very serious in his ask. I racked my brain to figure out if I had done anything wrong, but nothing came to mind. I was young, and I was naive, so I was very concerned about the meeting. What came next was advice that I have followed ever since he spoke his guiding words. He shared with me that the company wasn't doing well and that he had recently started the search process for a new position. The overall job market wasn't very good, but he was having a particularly difficult time finding a job because his skills were too highly specialized; what he brought to the table was too narrow. He counseled me not to do what he had done. He encouraged me to shape my career by being extremely broad in scope, with the goal being to gain as much knowledge and experience as possible in all aspects of business. He told me that I had a lot of potential, and that I should try to take advantage of as many opportunities as I was presented with to expand my areas of expertise. Knowing that nothing is irrevocable, he encouraged me to take calculated risks.

His professional heart-to-heart advice allowed me to comprehend in my twenties what he didn't discover until he was in his fifties. Having intentionally nurtured a diverse combination of depth and breadth of expertise and proficiency has been worth its weight in gold. I am eternally grateful to him for his candor and generosity. To this day, those powerful mentorship lessons so many years ago have permitted me to regularly add value in all aspects of my life.

Living our fast-paced lives, we are so wrapped up in our own day-to-day grind that we often forget about those around us who have had an impact on us personally, professionally, or in some cases both. Many of us think about them and give thanks as part of the end-of-year holiday season. Thinking about gratitude only once a year overlooks the immense benefit of utilizing it daily, especially in a business context. Employees are motivated by being recognized and praised by their manager. No one feels good when they are being taken for granted. When we assume recognition isn't necessary, it is an oversight that oftentimes has negative consequences. I would encourage you to take the time to express your appreciation. It doesn't cost us anything to offer a heartfelt "thank you." I have met people who are so uncomfortable verbalizing their gratitude that they justify not doing it. It takes both practice and courage to vocalize this kind of sincere acknowledgment.

Appreciation is a learned skill. Some of us may never have had the opportunity to acquire the awareness and respect for this reflective competence. Others may have predetermined, rigid opinions, or a narrow outlook, or may be afraid to change. We can increase our joy in life by adjusting our focus to appreciate what we already have rather than by being downhearted with what we don't have in our lives. When we learn to feel more comfortable with flexing a different mind-muscle by appreciating and expanding our gratitude skills, our brains are refocused to view people anew.

It is helpful to reflect back over your days, weeks, months and years, and even your lifetime, to consider any and all positive things that have happened; things that you are grateful for. We often forget to appreciate the various experiences and the assemblage of knowledge we've combined to produce the fabric of our lives. That know-how adds to your toolbox of cognition that you can utilize for your forward traction. Look back with gratitude on those people who have added significance to your life: a teacher, a boss, a co-worker, a fellow student, a coach, a guidance counselor, a college advisor, a family member, a friend, a neighbor, a significant other, or even a total stranger. I would encourage you to find a way to reach out to them. It is never too late to recognize their efforts on your behalf. If you discover that you neglected to thank someone for being especially kind or helpful, there is no time better than the present to try to connect with that person who helped you along your way in life. Remembering those individuals who have added worth to your life is powerful.

Shortly before a sinkhole caused my husband to fall off of a ladder and break his back, we had committed to doing a Warrior Dash charity event with a large group of family and a few friends. As much as he wanted to participate, he was physically incapable of doing so. I decided to still join in even though my athletic husband would be relegated to watching from the sidelines – not an easy thing for him to do. I was not in my best physical shape because I hadn't had the time to train, but I was bound and determined to finish the trek in the mud for this worthy cause. I started out strong until I reached a massive area of deep mud. I kept a positive mindset even though I was physically struggling. My goal was to battle through the rest of the obstacles to at least finish the mud run. My plan worked well until I got to the second to last obstacle, which was a three-story-high jungle gym type of netting. At about the halfway point, just as I was working my way up the front side, I heard a large group of college-age guys coming up fast and furiously on my heels. It was at that moment that something took place that I had never experienced before: I froze in fear. After what had happened to my husband just a few months earlier, I realized that I was petrified of falling from that height and getting seriously injured. By this time, the ropes were convulsing because of the volume of people who were going over this hurdle all at the same time. I knew that a number of my extended family members were waiting for me on the other side, but I was powerless to execute this part of the course. It was at this crucial point in time that I heard the words "I'm scared!" tumble out of my mouth. One of the college guys who was next to me immediately stopped climbing and said, "Don't worry, I will help you get over this. I've got you," and he did. He, along with a few family members, helped me to continue the rest of the way up and then safely down the other side. I remember jumping to the ground and feeling such relief as well as accomplishment. It was only after that bevy of emotions had subsided that I started to tear up with an incredible sense of gratitude. I realized that this complete stranger had sacrificed finishing the race with his friends so that he could help me. He showed up as an exceptional leader of his own life by supporting me through what felt like a life-and-death moment. I am eternally grateful that he had the courage as well as the kindness to stay behind and help me through my predicament. From the depth of my heart, I will always thank that awe-inspiring stranger.

It is easy to be grateful when our lives are going well. However, gratitude during hard times can be very difficult to contemplate.

During the murkiness of my most downbeat days, I have found myself melancholy and discouraged. My feelings of helplessness, disappointment, grief, pain, and disadvantage made me feel lonely and alone. I know how difficult it can be to look on the bright side when we are dealing with adversity, but wallowing in the contamination of self-pity never serves anyone well. When we lack gratitude, we can get locked into feelings of dissatisfaction instead of initiating a new attitude. I know how challenging it can be when my own cup has runneth over with strife, difficulties, and anxieties, but history has taught me that happiness is found on the other side. Instead of being inwardly focused on your own obstacles, try to shift your mindset to one of being encouraging and supportive of others. When our minds are available to engage in these hidden opportunities, we can instantly cultivate increases in coping, resilience, aptitude, and good fortune. This uplifting action is a gift for both the benefactor and the beneficiary. We know our own story, but we rarely know the detailed stories of those who are around us. Just like enthusiasm, gratitude can be contagious. To create a ripple effect of positive change, regularly model a grateful personality by getting into the habit of being thankful as well as appreciative. Commence a sequence of deliberate acts of kindness. Your gestures do not need to be grand as long as they are genuine. Some of us appreciate a private acknowledgment, others prefer more public praise, and some greatly appreciate a handwritten token of your gratitude. The energy and feeling behind your words is more esteemed than the perfection of the words themselves.

Top Nuggets of Wisdom

1 Gratitude opens our eyes to a more optimistic view of the world. Having an attitude of gratitude is a strength in character.

2 Thoughtful actions towards others play an active role in our physical health and well-being. Those of us that have an appreciative mindset are traditionally happier and have a greater degree of moral values.

3 Acts of gratitude provide personal benefit and motivation for the giver and the receiver.

CHAPTER 16

Call To Action

We are on the cusp of the end of traditional leadership. There are far too many outdated ideas about what leadership is. The competencies of the past are very different from what is needed to take us successfully into the future. With the brisk and brittle structure of our world today, the shortcomings in leadership are showing and growing.

Now is the time to take a stand and be the leader who starts the snowball of change in your orbit of influence. For a healthier tomorrow, we need to ignite an acceleration of leadership reform. This journey for foundational change starts with the power of one: one person, one action, one favorable result. The magnitude of one positive act is contagious and has a ripple effect on the world. If each of us commits to make a material difference each day with our regular interactions, the revolution for change will take hold.

Ethical citizenship compels us to participate daily in sustained efforts to bring about a greater society. I would like to believe that we can make traction to bridge the gaps so that we can better appreciate the factors that motivate the behavior of others, especially those that are contrary to our own views. With open hearts and minds, we can learn to appreciate diverse beliefs, traditions, and cultures. Stretch the limits of who you are. Gain new experiences by trying different things with different people. It is OK to feel uncomfortable; it's part of expanding yourself. Pushing through challenge is what makes us appreciate what is on the other side. If each of us is willing to stretch beyond our existing state of mind, it will create an upshot of beneficial results.

Err on the side of generosity rather than scarcity. If we resolve to focus on more acts of kindness, imagine the results we could accomplish together. Showing up as the leader you want to be, while inspiring others to do the same, will create a powerful force for the betterment of our world. Guide yourself and those in your sphere of influence with moral excellence and the courage to stay the course. Strive to achieve professional effectiveness and personal fulfillment.

Our earth must become more people-centric. We, the citizens, are the world's priceless treasure. When we are inspired, we create a chain reaction of enhanced energy and heightened results. Let's work together to shift our culture forward; let's accelerate a profound ripple effect of change. It is up to all of us to magnify our thinking and our actions.

Find your voice. Be open and agile. Seek wisdom. Think, feel, and speak your truth with integrity and respect. Practice empathy. Take pride in your own efforts. Create your purpose while adding value to those around you. Exhibit a distinctive presence with character and courage – shine on. We are braver, stronger, and smarter than we believe we are. Our world is just as beautiful and full of hope as it ever was. Live your best life! Humankind needs you.

Top Nuggets of Wisdom

1 The leadership competencies of the past are very different from what is needed to take us successfully into the future.

2 We are braver, stronger, and smarter than we believe we are.

3 Let's work together to shift our culture forward; let's accelerate a profound ripple effect of change.

Carpe Diem – Open Your Eyes and *LEAD!*

Author's Epilogue

When working with my leadership clients, I am often asked the same great question, so I thought I would share it with you in this Epilogue. Often the inquiry goes something like this:

> *I want to accelerate my success, but I don't know where to start. Is there a list that you can provide me with so that I can assess where I am today? I'd also like to understand what areas I should be focusing on for the future?*

Notable leaders are hard to find. They can look very different when they are exhibited in various circumstances and a myriad of personality styles. There is not a specific mold that accommodates every single leader in every possible leadership situation. Leadership is a melting pot of various skills, experiences, and abilities. To move towards excellence, here are some of the essential character traits and skills that the foremost leaders utilize as needed for the most effective outcomes.

Incomparable leaders:
- are humble, authentic, and transparent
- exemplify accountability, dependability, and sustainability
- make clear, impactful choices

- are exceptional communicators
- model relational intelligence by being approachable, collaborative, and reflective
- treat others with respect and consideration
- inspire loyalty, honesty, trust, and connection
- are fair, true to their word, and cleanly competitive
- seek out others to cover their blind spots
- are self-aware and have self-control
- develop the courage and wisdom to lead through adversity
- wade through conflicts and comprehend challenges
- find a smart balance between optimism and real-world solutions
- have a sense of purpose and an infectious passion to champion their vision
- give back and pay it forward
- commit to growing and mentoring others.

The best leaders in life are shaped by hardship and wisdom. As you embark upon your leadership journey, leverage your past to expand your future. I hope that many of the stories within the pages of this book will resonate with you, and that they will help you to continue to evolve as the consummate leader of your own life.

Social Media – An Invitation To Engage

Keywords: Open Your Eyes and Lead, Open Eyed Leadership, Leadership, Lead, Culture, Emotional Intelligence, Leadership Development, Innovation, CEO, Senior Leaders, Executives, Personal Excellence, Organizational Development, People Skills, Relationships, Work-Life Skills, Mindfulness, Empowerment, Personal Development, Lifestyle, Communications, Positive Change, Change Management, Motivational, Motivate, Inspirational, Inspire, Transformational, Traction, Grit, Perseverance, Results, Choices, Trailblazing, Kryptonite, Persevere, Empower, Excellence, Happiness, Courage, Impact, Purpose, Goals, Progress, Energy, Stretch, Expand, Achieve, Achievement, Change, Focus, Brand, Awareness, Success, Overcoming Hardship, Personal and Professional Obstacles

Twitter Feed: "Capistran empowers us to expand our thinking to balance and manage the omnipresent tensions while striving for leadership excellence."

For business, book groups, and other sharing opportunities: "The trajectory of leadership has been stifled due to the demands of our modern world. Circumstances are never the same, and change is all around us. As the needs of our society expedite, it is impairing the overall quality of leadership in our world. Profit drives business. Leaders require quicker, better, faster, and cheaper results, so they are squeezing wherever possible. Some even take the low road instead of the high road just to get ahead or stay ahead. When we are rushed for results, we tend to skim-coat our actions, which leads to diluted, lower-quality effort and results. Those involved feel tired and stressed, and over time become unengaged. Leaders that model integrity, excellence, fortitude, and kindness consistently create value and the biggest impact."

For high-value speaking engagements: "Nancy believes wholeheartedly in her book's content. Her goal is to make our world a better place through her real-life stories, concepts, ideas, and advice. Her enthusiasm allows her to create deep one-to-one personal connections with audiences of any size. With a style that is approachable and down to earth, she inspires people to become laser focused on taking action and making traction. Nancy can be reached at nancy@capistranleadership.com."

Acknowledgments

To continue to broaden our horizons, I believe it is important to make the time on a regular basis to read. Taking the time to digest the words in a well-written work of non-fiction is powerful. It allows us the opportunity to continue to develop our knowledge, our skills, and our abilities. It supports us in funneling our focus and boosting our productivity, allowing us to make smarter decisions with better precision. Thank you for choosing to invest your time and energy reading the pages of *Open Your Eyes and* LEAD. I hope the book supports you on your journey towards a fulfilling future.

I am extremely fortunate to be surrounded by colleagues, clients, friends, and family who continue to help me grow on a daily basis. While I would love to mention everyone by name, the list is too extensive, and there is always the chance that I would forget someone who I should have mentioned! Instead, I would like to thank everyone who has added value to the quality and traction of *Open Your Eyes and* LEAD.

To all of my past, current, and future clients – thank you for allowing me the opportunity to support you. I have intentionally not mentioned specific names or companies out of respect and confidentiality, but I thank you from the bottom of my heart for all that I learned from our experiences together.

To all of the like-minded trusted advisors of USA500 Clubs – thank you for the collaboration and ongoing support. Most notably: Tobe Gerard, Jonathan Tamkin, Lew Segall, Joe Chatham, Bill Jarry, and Rudy Scarito.

To Tara Goodwin – our instant connection fostered our friendship, and then our commonalities magnetized our business partnership. I believe that our bond formed quickly because of our similar personalities, experiences, intellect, and interests – what a powerful combination. Our united front has carried us through some great accomplishments together. I look forward to the journey ahead. Thank you for all that you do, especially for your warm introduction to Ken Lizotte.

To Ken Lizotte – I am grateful for your efforts in connecting me to Tracey Dobby. Thank you for helping me to navigate the initial stages of these uncharted waters.

To Tracey Dobby and Eclipse Publishing & Media – thank you for taking a leap of faith in me and my passion for enhancing the quality of leadership in our world. It is an amazing feat for a new author to professionally publish a book. Thank you for your open collaboration and commitment to a high-quality outcome. You have helped me to make my dream come true!

To Tobe Gerard – my dear friend – with the deepest of gratitude for believing in me and for the extensive efforts you put forth into editing my manuscript. You have been an amazing sounding board as

I went through this "new author" undertaking. You helped to bring organization and clarity to my words. You encouraged me to regularly dig deeper, which provided for a better-quality version of *Open Your Eyes and* LEAD. Your honesty and insights were invaluable, and I have appreciated them immensely. The deep bond that we organically created throughout this experience is well beyond anything I could have ever imagined. I hold you in the highest of regard. Our journey together has created a very special imprint in the deepest part of my heart.

To Mary McCann – you are such a cherished friend. I've respected and admired you since the first day we said "hello." We have gone through many stages of our lives together, and we have created an infinite amount of memories. Whenever my life got blurry along the way, you helped me to adjust my lens. Your friendship has given me the courage to grow in ways that I never imagined possible. The robust, high-quality bond of our over 35-year friendship has been essential to me. Thank you for feeding my soul and believing in me throughout the years.

To my Aunt Louise Beauchesne – thank you for being a lifeline for me as I battled through the most intense times due to our shared genetic predisposition. Your kindness, your generosity of time, your unwavering empathy, and your openness in sharing your journey with me were a beacon of light that guided my own journey.

To my parents, Jeannine and Richard Lacerte – thank you for your commitment to raising all five of us in the best way you knew how. Instilling your moral compass into us at a young age was a value add that I have benefited from as I've traveled through my life.

To the most important people in my life – my immediate family – I want and need to convey my profound gratitude. To my husband, Mark, to my son, Andrew, and to my daughter, Jennifer, I am forever gleeful knowing that you are a special part of my life. Through laughter, smiles, fears, and tears, the strength of our family bond has sustained the years. You have each been above and beyond patient with me as I carved out thousands of hours to write this book. I know how dramatically it impacted our quality time together, and going forward I promise that I will make it up to you. Your support during this journey into the unknown has been beyond priceless. Thank you for tolerating my intense commitment to nurture my dream of publishing this book in an effort to make a positive change in our world from a leadership perspective. Your steadfast love and devotion mean the world to me.

About The Author

Nancy Capistran, PCC, CPC

Nancy is an award-winning, internationally certified executive coach, motivational speaker, and trusted advisor. She is also the founder of three start-ups. Currently she is Principal of Capistran Leadership, LLC, and Crisis Interception, LLC.

She knows firsthand about extreme, abrupt, and unpredictable life experiences. Her bird's-eye view comes from being in the trenches and at the frontlines of several of life's most challenging times. Her "rebound-ability" has helped her to develop tried and true street-smart approaches to make traction and thrive through intensity. She brings thoughtful, visionary, and intelligent approaches that are grounded in real-world solutions. She has a contagious positive mental outlook with a spirit of steel. Nancy is often referred to as "911" for senior-level leaders.

For the past three decades, Nancy has held a wide range of positions and responsibilities in the specialty areas of corporate risk, compliance, and ethics; strategic planning and implementation; global crisis management; international program management; business administration and operations management; talent management; organizational development; retail/wholesale management; plus sales, service, marketing, procurement, new product development, manufacturing, and finance.

Nancy holds a BSBA from Northeastern University, a Master's Certification in Project Management (GWCPM) from George Washington University, and a Certificate in Leadership from Boston University. She is an accredited Professional Certified Coach (PCC) through the International Coaching Federation (ICF). She is also a Certified Professional Coach (CPC) and a Certified Energy Leadership Master Practitioner (ELI-MP) through the Institute for Professional Excellence in Coaching (iPEC), one of the largest ICF-accredited coach training schools in the world. Additionally, Nancy is a graduate of the Federal Bureau of Investigation's (FBI) Citizens Academy, and an active member of the Alumni Association.

www.capistranleadership.com – Capistran Leadership, LLC
www.nancycapistran.com – *Open Your Eyes and* LEAD